EDUCATION FOR
CONTINUITY
& CHANGE

EDUCATION FOR CONTINUITY & CHANGE

A NEW MODEL FOR CHRISTIAN RELIGIOUS EDUCATION

88-168

MARY ELIZABETH MOORE

Abingdon Press / Nashville

Education for Continuity and Change:
A New Model for Christian Religious Education

Copyright © 1983 by Abingdon Press

Library of Congress Cataloging in Publication Data

MOORE, MARY ELIZABETH, 1945–
    Education for continuity and change.
    Bibliography: p.
    Includes index.
    1. Christian education—Philosophy. I. Title.
BV1464.M66   1983   207   82-13901

ISBN 0-687-11523-X

MANUFACTURED BY THE PARTHENON PRESS AT
NASHVILLE, TENNESSEE, UNITED STATES OF AMERICA

To my mother and father,

Elizabeth Heaton and James Ogle Mullino,

who have given me the gift of life, introduced me to the traditioning community, and cared for me, even at the roughest intersections. I thank them for sharing themselves with me as parents and wise companions.

Contents

Preface

Many times in my life I have wondered whether I could change a particular attitude or behavior. I have struggled with the apparent tension between continuity and change in making decisions. I have recognized the necessity for courageously risking a change, but I have known the folly in ignoring both past heritage and future vision. Often, too, I have wondered if the church could possibly be transformed itself and if it could have any real impact on the world, which knows so much suffering and injustice. This history has led me finally to this book.

The search for a new model of Christian religious education is at the heart of this book. The hope is for a new model that does not pull continuity and change apart but recognizes how inextricably bound they are. The use of the phrase *Christian religious education* is awkward, to say the least. Its awkwardness may reflect the crisis of identity in the discipline—the pull between those who call themselves religious educators and those who prefer to be identified as Christian educators. Using the term *Christian religious education* communicates that the search for a new model is one that is taking place within the Christian faith community and, at the same time, one that is shared in many ways by religious educators in other faith communities. For these reasons, I join other recent educators who have chosen to use the cumbersome *Christian religious education* to describe our endeavor.

I express gratitude to some of those communities and

persons who have made this book possible. I am grateful to the School of Theology at Claremont, which I have known both as a student and as a faculty member. The faculty here has stimulated and challenged me, and the students have never ceased to open new vistas for my thought. I appreciate also the fellowships that have nurtured me—the many youth and adults with whom I have journeyed and the congregations that have supported and guided me.

I express particular gratitude to my faculty colleagues who have extensively dialogued with me about this book—John Cobb, Paul Irwin, and Philip Dreyer. Thanks to their wise companionship along the way.

My deepest gratitude goes to my family, who have endured, cared, and kept me human. My parents, Elizabeth and James Mullino, have never ceased to believe in me, even when I know they were tempted to do so. My children, Cliff and Rebecca, are living reminders of the importance of the church's educational mission, and they are persons who have cared for me and allowed me to care for them. Also, Joyce, Nan, and Glenda have offered valuable support and interest, for which I am grateful. Finally, I thank my husband, Allen Moore, for being a challenging colleague and close companion. His ideas were always provocative, and his encouragement and homemaking were invaluable.

In expressing appreciation to these groups and persons, I am aware that the way their influences have been brought together is my responsibility. Any inadequacies in this book, therefore, are my own.

1 SEEKING A NEW MODEL

Setting the Stage

Once upon a time God created.

> In the beginning God created the heavens and the earth. The earth was without form and void, and darkness was upon the face of the deep; and the Spirit of God was moving over the face of the waters. (Gen. 1:1-2)

Once upon a time God redeemed.

> Now the birth of Jesus Christ took place in this way. When his mother Mary had been betrothed to Joseph, before they came together she was found to be with child of the Holy Spirit; and her husband Joseph, being a just man and unwilling to put her to shame, resolved to divorce her quietly. But as he considered this, behold, an angel of the Lord appeared to him in a dream, saying, "Joseph, son of David, do not fear to take Mary your wife, for that which is conceived in her is of the Holy Spirit; she will bear a son, and you shall call his name Jesus, for he will save his people from their sins." (Matt. 1:18-21)

Once upon a time God moved on the earth—creating and redeeming. In God's creating was redemption, and in God's redeeming was creation. God moved on the earth, and the earth has never been the same. And God continues to move, creating and redeeming, pulling the world toward the Kingdom.

Once upon a time is captivating language. The words transport us into another world, a world that is past but still is. When we hear the words, we know that a story that is real will follow because it is a tale of once in a part of time. The story becomes the bearer of a culture, the story of a people. The big story is the saga of God's people. This saga is a traditional history of our community, and it enters into our lives as we enter into it. In the interaction the saga has power to shape our being and our future. Likewise the saga is shaped by us as we hear it, tell it, and live in it. It is a growing story.

The Christian community, in all its longing for relevance and influence on the contemporary world, must recognize that its story is ancient. The same community, in its longing for the stability of long-established truths, must recognize the dynamic way in which its story is told, interpreted, and transformed.

The Problem

And so we are plunged into the tension between continuity and change, between historical tradition and contemporary experience. The history of religious education involves shifts in emphasis between these two. The concern for continuity has been paired with an emphasis on historical tradition, and the concern for change has been paired with an emphasis on contemporary experience. The proponents of one viewpoint have often assumed that the other viewpoint has been overly stressed or taken for granted in the church or the society. The problem with this assumption is that an important corrective emphasis during one period becomes a one-sided emphasis for another time and situation. Furthermore, neither viewpoint gives much attention to the future. If we take seriously the work of Latin American liberation theologians and theologians of hope, we must recognize that this de-emphasis on the future represents a distortion of the Christian faith.

The tension between continuity and change has been a part of the Jewish and Christian communities throughout their history. For example, the Old Testament prophets appealed to their own experience of God, to their context, and to the historical tradition of Israel as their sources of authority.[1] The test of true prophecy was, not an appeal to tradition or experience, but the rightness of the text and its interpretation when speaking the Word of God in a particular context. Sanders recognizes that for the prophet to discern the Word of God for a particular moment in history the prophet must have "both intimate knowledge of the traditions or 'texts' of the ways of God in Israel's past (her *mythos* or Torah story), and a dynamic ability to perceive the salient facts of one's own moment in time as they move through the fluidity of history."[2] The challenge comes, however, in having that detailed knowledge of both the traditional text and the contemporary context and in sensing the fresh meaning of a given text for a given context. James Sanders recognizes our difficulty in modern times of understanding "what the canonical prophets meant by listening to the voice of God (Jer. 7:23, 26), or what the Reformers meant by interpretation by or through the Holy Spirit."[3] This cannot be ignored, however, in facing the challenge of relating the text to the context.

This one challenge has long been recognized, the challenge of determining the meaning of the historical text for changing contexts. Another challenge must also be recognized, however, and this promises to be more controversial. This is the challenge of seeking fresh meanings in the present moment that add something new to the tradition. This, no less than the first challenge, calls us to discern the voice of God.

In saying this we recognize the contribution of both the historical tradition and contemporary experience to the saga of God's people. An arbitrary choice between the two seems neither possible nor desirable. But the Judeo-Christian communities have always been plagued with this tension between the historical tradition and contemporary experience and with the temptation to choose between the two emphases. Furthermore, the temptation has been to ignore future expectations and hopes altogether.

The tension between past and present has risen again to the forefront of discussion since Schleiermacher.[4] This tension has been at the heart of many theological debates, for example, the mid-twentieth-century debate between liberal Christianity and neo-orthodoxy and the corresponding debate between progressive religious education and the neo-orthodox formulation of Christian education. The theologians of hope and liberation theologians have called fresh attention to the third element in the tension, future hope. Jürgen Moltmann, for example, has argued that future hope offers the guiding focus for our faith, for God is future and is revealed in the event of promise. This emphasis on future is beginning to impact Christian religious education, particularly through the work of Thomas Groome.

The basic issue arising out of this for systematic theology is: How does the religious community live in faithfulness to its past (continuity) and in openness to its present and future (change)? This raises fundamental questions as to how God is revealed and where the authority of the religious community lies. Is the authority of the Christian faith in the contemporary experience of persons in the world where God is immanent? Is it in the Word of God as revealed and recorded in the Bible or in the Christian church tradition? Or is it in the eschatological hope revealed in God's promises? Further, is the Christian story one that is already fully revealed and that we, therefore, seek to understand so we can live in continuity with it? Or is the Christian story not finished yet and, therefore, continually open to new revelation and new interpretation?

The questions in Christian religious education have been closely related to these. The questions concern what to teach, how, and why. Is the content of Christian religious education the biblical and historical church tradition, the contemporary experience of the Christian community and the world, or the hoped for Kingdom of God? Should the method transmit that tradition or enable the creative interpretation and reconstruction of present experience? Should the purpose be to maximize the continuity of the Christian community or to maximize the potential for change? Or for any of these questions, is the answer somewhere in between?

The desire to transcend the continuity/change dualism is not new in religious education. George Albert Coe urged the importance of both tradition and creativity in education,[5] but his own work leaned heavily in the direction of the creative dimension. Since Coe's time, the pendulum has continued to swing. In recent years mediating points of view have emerged, but more has been done to highlight the tension than to resolve it. Some answers have been posed, and some new questions have emerged. These will be explored in chapter 2.

The Purpose

The purpose of this book will be to propose a model of education that maximizes both continuity and change. This promises to be no small task, especially in light of the historical tendency to set the two in opposition to one another.

The assumption underlying this model is that a theory of Christian religious education should explain and stimulate both continuity and change. We need to call into question our dualistic way of thinking, our assumption that continuity rules change and vice versa. We need, instead, to see the possibility that the more a person is continuous with the past, the greater are the possibilities for change, and the more he or she changes, the more that person is continuous with the past. This may sound absurd because dualistic thinking is dominant in our culture. However, our task is to overcome such thinking.

The traditioning model that will be proposed here offers a fresh perspective for Christian religious education. The concept of traditioning is based on the idea that the Christian community lives in its tradition, passing on its past, living in its present, and moving toward its future. It is ever linked to its past but is never static. Continuity and change are always tied together.

The traditioning model is quite different from a socialization (or enculturation) model that encourages the continuity of the community through socializing persons into the community's beliefs, values, and practices. It is likewise different from a reconstructionist model that emphasizes the changing of the community through reflection on and revision of one's actions. The former tends to ignore the ministry's prophetic element through which the community is critiqued and recognized as always inadequate to socialize persons for God's kingdom. The latter tends to be overly optimistic about the community's ability to critique itself and tends to ignore the priestly element through which the community remembers and celebrates God's gifts.

The traditioning model provides a new perspective and a pattern for the church's educational ministry, an attempt to be more adequate than either a socialization or a reconstructionist model. The traditioning model affirms what these other models affirm, i.e., the importance of passing on the community's beliefs, values, and practices and the importance of reflecting on and revising the community's actions. The traditioning model, however, is built on the idea that neither of these goals can be achieved separately from the other.

Both continuity and change are essential to the life of the Christian community. The phenomenon of continuity makes it possible for persons to enter into the life of the community, and the phenomenon of change provides for the community's openness to present experience and future possibility.

The word *model* is chosen to describe this undertaking because it is a description of educational ministry that provides a pattern for our actions. The concept of model is easiest to describe in the form of a story..

As everyone knows, most colleges and universities are troubled by persons who insist on wearing paths across the grass rather than walking on the sidewalks. The administrators of a new college vowed to avoid this perennial problem by delaying the pouring of sidewalks on the new college grounds. Classes began, and students and faculty walked across the dirt in whatever patterns they wished. After a year of such unguided walking, the college was marked with paths. The traffic patterns had taken a recognizable shape as paths were formed all across the grounds. The administrators then laid the sidewalks where the paths had been worn.

Let these sidewalks represent a model. Just as the sidewalks were laid according to the flow of traffic, the model is based on available data about education theory and practice. It is a description of what is known, a description as adequate as we can put forth. Just as the sidewalks will serve as a guide for walkers in the future, the educational model serves as a guide for those on the education journey. It is a pattern for our actions. Neither the sidewalks nor the model guarantee that no one will ever again walk on the grass or venture in new directions. They offer instead a pattern that is as adequate as we can envision at the present time.

A model, then, emerges as we reflect theoretically on educational practice and as we allow our reflections to guide our future practice. It is not an unchanging description, however, which conforms perfectly with nature. It is instead an explanation of experience that is always open to reconstruction in light of new experience, revelation, or analysis. One model cannot be the final word, nor can it take the place of all earlier models. It is, rather, a new perspective that describes and guides educational ministry.

What is needed now is a model of Christian religious education that maximizes persons' connectedness with the past so that the transformations taking place in their life will be rooted and will be all the richer. What is needed is a model that maximizes persons' changing so that their connectedness with the past will help them live in the changing world and with God's call forward. This calls for a model that opens persons to past, present, and future and to the interactions among these. This is a kind of opening up and bringing together that cannot be taken for granted, for it does not often happen without intentionality.

The purpose of this study is twofold: (a) to call attention to the need for education that creates openings to past, present, and future and maximizes their integration and (b) to offer a reformulation of Christian religious education theory and practice, a foundation for a new kind of educational ministry in the Christian community.

This is a particularly important need in a complex world in which the church lives among many pressures pulling in different directions. The church faces real temptations either to return to a simpler past or to change rapidly in order to be relevant to the times. Yielding to either is one-sided and inadequate.

What is needed in education is a renewed vision of how continuity and change exist in relationship. What is further needed is an educational model for stimulating both and enhancing this relationship. The purpose of this book will be to create such a vision and such a model.

The Promise of a New Model

So the task of this project is defined, with no less challenge than met Coe. The faith community cannot escape the influences of past, present, and future. The claim here is that the tension between continuity and change is resolved only when the artificial dichotomies are broken down and attempts at delicate balancing are abandoned. The tension is resolved when education maximizes both continuity and change so that the faith community can pass on, critique, and reform its tradition.

The model proposed here is one in which the central task is to involve persons in the living Christian tradition and is therefore called a traditioning model. Implicit in this is the idea that traditioning is an active process of passing down and reforming the historical tradition. The traditioning task in educational ministry has two dimensions: hermeneutics, or interpretation, and transformation. They are interrelated, and each is made possible by the other.

Hermeneutics is an opening up of persons to their past traditions, present experiences, and future expectations and hopes. Hermeneutics cannot, in fact, be done without an eye to the past out of which the Christian community lives and an eye to the future toward which that community moves. Education maximizes continuity and change when it facilitates the hermeneutical task. The educator is engaged in creating openings, i.e., in interpreting and in enabling others to interpret the historical Christian tradition, the contemporary experience of the faith community and the world, and Christian hope. Hermeneutics provides a bridge that links past, present, and future in the total life of the Christian community.

Transformation is a changing of persons and culture, a conversion. Transformation is a reforming of persons, of societies, and of the historical tradition itself. It is rooted in our historical traditions, in the dynamics of our present social situation, and in our vision. This means that we cannot hope for transformation if we deny our past or ignore our present situation or future hope. We are like the prophet Amos who reminded Israel of Yahweh's deliverance of them out of Egypt and of their unjust practices and warned them of Yahweh's impending judgment. This was not just a history lesson but a prophetic call for change.

Basic Concepts

A few key concepts will be explored in this book as we probe the apparent conflict between continuity and change. Continuity and change have often been paired respectively with emphases on tradition and on experience. These four concepts will be explored here as a prologue to the drama in which they play various roles and are viewed from different perspectives.

Continuity

Continuity is a state of connectedness in which parts form an unbroken chain through time and space. The continuity of the Christian community, which is the concern of this book, is reflected in the connectedness of the community's beliefs, practices, values, and stories through time and across the globe.

The radical claim here is that the community must recognize how deeply connected it is through time and across the globe. The claim moves sharply, against the to-each-one's-own approach to faith. Instead, it recognizes the importance of each person's linkage with people of the past and with those in other communities. Efforts to ignore this connectedness are made in certain individualistic political and social theories, but these efforts are illusory. For example, to suppose that what is consumed in one part of the world does not affect the economy and the availability of food in other parts of the world is to ignore political realities.

Change

Change is the opposite of continuity in that it is a transformation, conversion, or reversal that breaks into the connectedness in some way. Change is an action of making something different or of becoming different. It includes deviation from normative patterns of beliefs, practices, values, and stories. In the Christian community change takes place in each generation and in different parts of the globe as persons read the past from inside their own unique sociohistorical contexts and as novelty is introduced into these situations through the inbreaking of God.

The radical claim in this book is that change is so much a part of the world that neither persons nor the church as a whole are ever static. The idea that either is unchanging or even has an unchanging core is rejected along with the idea that Christian truth is in any way static. Tradition, then, does not embody static truth that is applied in different situations. Christian tradition is ongoing, and the truth it reflects never stands still. Neither do persons or the church, which participate in it.

Tradition

Tradition is a handing over, or passing down, of the good news. It is initiated by God's gifts that are passed on through the community's beliefs, practices, values, and stories. These traditions are characteristically communicated at first by oral transmission through the community's life. They generally provide norms that are rooted in the past and that guide the Christian community in the present.

Here we are distinguishing among Tradition (what God gives, or hands over), tradition (the process by which this gift is passed on), and traditions (the vehicles of communication). The concept of tradition might not seem so objective and immutable to some or so oppressive to others if we make this distinction. Traditions often become equated with Tradition, and God's actions get reduced to human proportions. If these traditions were seen, instead, as windows for God's gifts (Tradition) and vehicles for communicating these to others, then the real depth and power of tradition could be appreciated more fully.

What, then, is the meaning of the tradition process (traditioning)? It is initiated by God's gift and revelation. The gift is then witnessed to and handed down.[6] It is to be received and preserved and has transforming power.[7] This suggests that the process of tradition embodies both continuity and change. The community preserves the gift and the witness to it, but the gift and the witness change that community. Furthermore, the community continues to interact with God and the world so that its witness never stands still. God continues to act, and the community is continually reformed. The community's emphasis may vary between preservation and transformation, but both are essential to the nature of tradition.

Yves Congar likens the tradition process to a delivery system initiated by God's acts and continued through Christ, the early church, and the contemporary church.[8] Tradition, then, is the chief example of the interdependence of human persons. Persons deliver the tradition to one another, mediating the divine to one another. Congar emphasizes the significance of this.

> We can bring about our own death, but we cannot give ourselves life. In the closed world of living creatures, species even live on one another, and the balance of the whole system is assured by the cooperation of the individual parts— it is a vast web, a seamless garment. In the normal course of events we receive our faith from another; we cannot baptize ourselves. Thus, it is normal for persons to depend on one another in order to achieve their supernatural destiny.[9]

This tradition process, then, has both horizontal (person-to-person, community-to-community) and vertical (persons-to-God) dimensions. It includes all God's communication to humanity and the ongoing transmission of that communication.[10] This is the meaning intended in this study.

The word *traditioning* is used here to distinguish between tradition as a process and traditions. Traditioning is the process of handing over God's gifts from one person to another, and traditions are the vehicles by which this is done. The distinction between Scripture and tradition, which has at times been controversial in Christian history, will not be dealt with here. The concept of traditions is being used in a more generic sense. Traditions are taken to include Scripture, doctrine, rituals, and stories. They include any communication of the good news that has been part of Christian history.

Experience

Experience, like tradition, is both a process and the result of process. It is the process of observing, participating in, or living through events. In the Christian community, then, one could say that persons experience the events of their life together and of their world. Persons also experience their own thoughts and feelings, and they experience other persons' stories in the form of written documents and oral transmission. The Bible, for example, is a record of human experience in all these dimensions: historical events, internal stirrings of the soul, and rituals, myths, and stories. What is more, the Bible comes to us as a document to be reexperienced freshly.

We can also speak of experience as the collective wisdom, knowledge, and skills of a person or a community. This way of speaking of experience is cumulative, resulting from living through many particular experiences and anticipating others. We can, therefore, speak of the Christian community's experience, and this would include its historical traditions, its present experiences of God and the world, and its expectations for the future.

These dimensions of the meaning of experience give some sense of the richness of the concept. Its usage in religious education literature has often been more limited. The emphasis has usually been on the role of present experience in education and has been twofold. It has included emphases on student-centered education (which finds its starting point in the personal experiences of the students) and on field-based, or laboratory, education (which focuses on the educational value of learning by doing and by relating to others). An attempt will be made here to enlarge these emphases to include not only the personal and field-based experiences, but also the cultural, historical, and future dimensions of experience. These cultural, historical, and future dimensions shape persons and the way in which they experience events in the present. Likewise the events of the present influence the way persons experience culture, history, and future expectations.

In these definitions, one can already see that tradition, though rooted in the past, cannot be limited to the past because it is an ongoing process of passing on and moving toward future. Tradition is continually being formed and re-formed. One can also see that experience, though related to events of the present, includes the past and the anticipations of future. One might also recognize, however, that the educational focus has often been on the historical tradition or the contemporary experience, and the dualism between these two has been perpetuated by the failure to recognize the fullness of either. This failure has been heightened by the tendency to ignore the future altogether.

The Task

The attempt in this book is to address the dualism between historical tradition and contemporary experience and to move beyond it. Though the dualism itself is false, it is so deeply ingrained that it requires thoroughgoing analysis. Every time the dualism is stated a certain irony will be communicated, as the so-called duality is not, in fact, a duality at all.

Once dualistic thinking is overcome, it becomes clear that the greatest faithfulness to historical tradition is found in the most dynamic creativity in the present, creativity in which past, present, and future meet. This is the challenge before us here.

This study is an attempt at model-building. The model will hopefully generate new images for the theory and practice of Christian religious education, images that are vital and that facilitate the traditioning of the faith communities. These communities stand in the present, rooted in past and pulled toward future. They have no choice but to move into the future. The hope implicit in the traditioning model is that the movement to future will be deeply informed by the past and present and that communities will be open to God's transforming power and to their own power as agents of transformation.

2

The Dilemma: Tradition and Experience in Christian Religious Education

> Mankind likes to think in terms of extreme opposites. It is given to formulating its beliefs in terms of *Either-Ors,* between which it recognizes no intermediate possibilities. When forced to recognize that the extremes cannot be acted upon, it is still inclined to hold that they are all right in theory but that when it comes to practical matters circumstances compel us to compromise. Educational philosophy is no exception.[1]

In 1938 John Dewey expressed dismay that educational philosophy was torn between traditional and progressive education. Traditional education was predominantly concerned with conveying the information, skills, and moral standards of the past to serve as a guide to persons in the present. Progressive education was primarily concerned with learning through experience and with encouraging persons in their self-expression, individuality, and free activity.

Dewey himself was a pioneer in progressive education, but he became increasingly concerned about the conception of educational theories in such dichotomies. The pendulum swings back and forth as new theories emerge in reaction against others. He set out to articulate an educational theory based on a philosophy of experience.[2] He saw such a theory as making the past relevant to the present and future and as escaping the unfortunate dichotomy between teaching the past and educating through experience.

The dualism that Dewey bemoaned is persistent in religious education as well. C. Ellis Nelson recognizes the tension between tradition and transformation as the oldest problem in religious eduation.[3] He, like Dewey, resists dichotomizing and insists on the dynamic relationship of tradition and experience in human lives.[4] Others in recent years have tackled this problem with similar concern, notably Thomas Groome, Mary Boys, Maria Harris, and Letty Russell.

A fuller understanding of the problem and possible clues for its resolution can be sought in the history of religious education. The problem can hardly be considered in isolation from that history. Neither can it be understood apart from the questions currently being asked in the practice of Christian education or the educational theories in which some synthesis of the poles is envisioned. The purpose in this chapter will be to add historical depth and practical theoretical breadth to our understanding of this problem of the duality between continuity and change and the potential resolutions.

Historical Shapes of Education

The focus here will be on twentieth-century movements in religious education, in which the tension between historical tradition and contemporary experience has been highlighted in many different ways. We have recognized in chapter 1 that tradition is ongoing, that it is not purely historical. We have also recognized that experience is cumulative, that it is not purely contemporary. For the purposes of this discussion, however, we will deal with the historical aspects of tradition and the contemporary aspects of experience. This is the way the dichotomy has often been set up, and throughout this study it will be referred to in terms of historical tradition and contemporary experience.

The twentieth-century educational debate between these two emphases grew out of earlier movements, so we are dealing with an issue that has long plagued Christian religious education. Notice that even the language is different on the two sides of the debate. In the early years the experiential side was often conceived of as *religious education* because the proponents were most concerned with the education of persons in the religious spirit and values. The traditional side was often conceived of as *Christian education* or *church education,* for proponents were more confessional in their interests and were concerned with educating persons into a particular understanding of the Christian faith.

On the Side of Experience

Since the seventeenth century educators have shown increasing concern with the role of present experience in education. Increased attention has been directed to experience, i.e., to those events that students have observed or participated in. This was a particular emphasis of the progressive religious education movement, which emerged alongside the progressive philosophy of education in the United States in the early twentieth century. Its influence was dominant in North American religious education until the 1950s and is still a force in religious education theory and practice. Progressive education was aimed at moving persons and society forward by stimulating people to think and live effectively through experiential educational methods. This philosophy of education influenced (and was influenced by) the thinking of George Albert Coe, William Clayton Bower, and other early leaders of the religious education movement.

Coe is often referred to as the father of the religious education movement. His basic understanding of Christian education was: "an experiment in being Christian, an experiment through which the meaning of 'Christian' unfolds to us."[5] He understood the goals of education to be social adjustment and the development of children's potential religious nature.[6] In keeping with these emphases, he called for student-centered education and placed emphasis on "learning by doing" and self-expression.[7] Coe's prevailing concern was experience: being aware of the previous experience of the students, designing educational experiences that would make contact with the needs and interests of persons at different ages, and building toward better forms of experience in the future.

Bower's philosophy of education was similar. He saw education as a creative process. Education was understood as initiation into a creative, social experience, and the goal of religious education was to help persons develop moral and spiritual qualities. Bower was writing a few years (twenty-five) after Coe had begun and further developed some of Coe's ideas. Bower's educational thrust, like Coe's, was experiential. He identified the educational process with the process of analyzing contemporary experience and of re-forming values and action. Past experience was important for reflecting on contemporary experience, but the starting point was the contemporary. Furthermore, attention was given to the education experience itself, which was intended to take place in a democratic social setting.[8]

Cultural Influences

This emphasis on the experiential, experimental, and processive nature of education did not arise in a vacuum. It was shaped in part by the particular cultural context in which it emerged. The context was early twentieth-century United States prior to World War I and the depression, a period of general optimism in this country. Industrial democracy was thought to be the institutional form that would re-create the world into an ideal social order. Many historical commentators speak of the progressive movement as a reflection of the western (particularly United States) liberal culture of the time. The turn of the century was a period of optimism about human nature and achievement. This was a period when the social gospel was influential with its naïve optimism about building God's kingdom on earth.

Furthermore, the early twentieth century was impacted by the emergence of biblical criticism that challenged the literal, transmissive biblical teaching of the day. The absolute authority of the Bible was brought into question, and interpretation came to be understood as complex rather than simple and obvious.

This was also a period when pragmatism, instrumentalism, and experimentalism were dominant in United States culture. The search for truth through experimentation had begun to emerge in the late sixteenth and early seventeenth centuries with Francis Bacon. Its general influence on culture culminated in the late nineteenth and early twentieth centuries in the United States with the pragmatism of Pierce, James, and Dewey. The consequences of this movement in education were a trend from deductive to inductive methods and an emphasis on learning from experience. Coe reflected this influence in his basic definition of Christian education as "an experiment in being Christian." Bower's experimental emphasis was evident in his educational method in which persons studied the content of their own experience and made decisions about action in light of probable outcomes.

Historical Influences Within Educational Theory

In addition to the dominant ideas and ethos in the United States, several historical developments in educational thought influenced the emerging experiential emphases in education. Three streams of thought that were particularly influential will be discussed here.

Developmental processes in human life. Increasing recognition was being given to the developmental processes in human life. Some of the persons who first called attention to this, in the seventeenth and eighteenth centuries, were Comenius, Rousseau, and Pestalozzi. Friedrich Froebel took their ideas to natural conclusions with his emphasis on child-centered education suited to the natural development of the students. He advocated such things as the use of games and play as educational methods. Modern kindergarten education has been shaped under the influence of his ideas.

In the mid-nineteenth century, religious institutions were being impacted to some extent by the developmental ideas of a few people like Horace Bushnell. He emphasized helping persons grow as Christians through nurturing experiences in the church and home. He wanted children to be brought up "in conversion," and his often-quoted thesis was "that the child is to grow up a Christian, and never know himself as being otherwise."[9] He emphasized that worship, play, and family experiences of all kinds have an important role in the nurture of children and their learning, even before full cognitive development.

The developmental focus in general education came to a new culmination in John Dewey in the early twentieth-century United States. He suggested that education itself is a process and that persons develop in continuous, never-ending ways. The impact of Dewey and of these earlier educational theorists was felt strongly in the progressive religious education movement of the twentieth-century United States. The most obvious impact was a radical shift in attention to the natural processes of students and a consequent shift to student-centered education. Religious education came to be seen as the facilitation of persons' development through age-appropriate experiences rather than instruction in the information and values of the past. Developmental theory came to be used by Coe and others as a "point of contact" with the students of different ages.

God-human relatedness. A second stream of thought influencing experiential education was an increasing interest in the God-human relationship. This emerged in two different ways. Comenius (seventeenth century) held a mystical view of the divine-human unity. He was followed by two other similarly viewed shapers of educational thought: Friedrich Froebel and Ralph Waldo Emerson. Alongside this mystical stream of thought was the evolution of natural theology. John Locke advocated natural theology in the late seventeenth century, and Henry Nelson Wieman, in this century, stressed the seeking of God's work in the natural order.

The implications of these trends for the progressive religious education movement were an optimism about God's being revealed in and through the world and a consequent turning of attention to human relationships in which God was understood to be present. Both Coe and Harrison Elliott stressed divine immanence and, with the assumptions of natural theology, spoke of religious education. These emphases led educators to see human experience as the central content of education.

Educational value of ordinary experience. At the same time, increasing attention was being given to the educational value of ordinary experience. Benjamin Franklin, for example, advocated practical education in all areas of life, and Pestalozzi and others stressed experiential models of education. In the twentieth century this stream of thought was further influenced by the increasing sophistication of psychological learning theory. From this emerging body of theory came the emphasis on problem-solving as a contributor to learning and on the importance of applying ideas in practice.[10]

Dewey addressed this issue in his writing and in his school where he stressed the role of social experience in education. Under his guidance in the laboratory-school at the University of Chicago, teaching was accomplished through active participation in the various fields of study. The consequences of this development for religious education were, again, a movement away from transmissive education and increased attention to experiential education. The starting point for religious education came to be the life situation, and even the resources of the Bible and tradition were approached only through contemporary real-life problems. This was particularly emphasized by Harrison Elliott in the 1940s.

On the Side of Tradition

The shapes of religious education reviewed above emerged largely in opposition to then-prevalent educational modes in which the stress was on transmitting the historical tradition, or the heritage of the past. Comenius, Rousseau, Pestalozzi, Froebel, Bushnell, Dewey, Coe, and Bower were considered radical in their educational thinking because they called for emphases that were alien to the educational practices of their day. Though these shapers of education have radically impacted twentieth-century understandings of education, the dominant educational forms in religious communities continue to be centered around transmitting the knowledge and values of the past.

Twentieth-Century Shapers

In the early twentieth century the Sunday school movement was still largely characterized by tradition-based education. Later emerged theorists who laid foundations for neo-orthodox interpretations of Christian education in Protestantism and for the kerygmatic renewal in Roman Catholic catechesis.

Sunday school movement. The Sunday school movement was launched in England in the late eighteenth century (the date is usually set at 1780). From its inception the movement was designed to provide young people with something they were lacking. In its beginning the Sunday school was to be a place for young boys to go during idle hours, an opportunity to learn to read and write, and an opportuity to learn about the Bible and to become Christian. The movement began as a response to human need, i.e., the need for poor boys to occupy their leisure time constructively and to learn what they had no opportunity to learn elsewhere. At this same time, the movement was focused more on transmitting the accumulated skills and knowledge of the past than on helping these young men interpret their experiences.

Certain characteristics of the Sunday school movement illustrate this point further. First, it was an evangelizing movement, and this was never truer than on the frontier in the United States. The goals of the movement, at that time, were to prepare persons for conversion and for death, so persons were taught primarily about salvation and judgment.[11] The emphasis on conversion continued in the movement, so salvation continued to be a teaching theme. The content in later years, however, shifted away from judgment themes and focused more on what was understood as basic biblical teaching.[12] The evangelizing thrust continued, and with missionary zeal leaders of the movement began to look toward the whole world as the frontier of the Sunday school. What was being carried around the world, in fact, was Christianity as understood in the civil religion of Great Britain and the United States.[13]

A second characteristic of the Sunday school movement was its emphasis on unity and uniformity. Being an ecumenical Protestant movement, it was designed to teach those essential principles and ideas of Christianity on which all Protestants agreed. Sunday school teaching in the early 1900s was based on the Uniform Lesson Plan in which these basic principles and ideas were set forth in an orderly way. As noted above, these essential principles and ideas were often identifiable with civil religion.

A third characteristic of the movement, was its emphasis on teaching the subject matter. Kathan notes: "The Bible has been the central course of instruction from the beginning, and where it is not, parents and others question its [the Sunday school's] validity."[14] These emphases on the subject matter and on the design of the Uniform Lesson Plan itself were criticized by some of the professional religious educators of the era. One dominant criticism was that the same material was taught to everyone and developmental differences in needs and experiences were largely ignored. Robert Lynn and Elliott Wright point out in their history of the Sunday school that the leaders of the movement did, in fact, treat children as little adults until early in the twentieth century.[15] Note, however, that this orientation to purely traditional subject matter and this neglect of human-life experiences began to change as early as 1920. In this year William Bower's International Lesson Committee produced a curriculum that broadened the subject matter to include social interaction and life experience.

A fourth characteristic of this Sunday school movement was its being a lay movement. It was begun and continued by laypersons, and it was only domesticated by American churches in the middle years of the last century. This would suggest that until rather late in its history the Sunday school was separated from the experiential life of the church in worship, mission, and so forth. This often continued, even after the Sunday schools were taken over by the churches. Some of the faith community's experiences were not, then, available to its content or to its scope of influence. In fact, on the United States frontier, the Sunday school often preceded both churches and public schools in new settlements, so it was often considerably isolated from many experiences of congregational life.

Neo-orthodox and kerygmatic approaches to Christian education. Early in this century the Sunday school movement was influenced by progressive religious education, but tradition-oriented modes began to emerge in the middle of the century. In Protestantism H. Shelton Smith argued strongly from a neo-orthodox point of view against experiential education, and in Roman Catholicism Josef A. Jungmann and Johannes Hofinger urged the teaching of tradition with particular emphasis on the "central core of the message we are to proclaim."[16] Both neo-orthodoxy and the kerygmatic renewal were Christocentric. Both of these movements were opposed to traditionalism for its own sake. Rather than being concerned with the communication of every jot and tittle from the historical tradition, advocates in both movements were concerned that persons encounter the living reality of Christ through that tradition. This was not for the sake of knowing details of the biblical or historical account, but for the sake of living a Christian life.

Interestingly enough, Jungmann and Hofinger were not themselves reacting against experiential education but against a more extreme form of tradition-based education that did not separate the essential doctrines from the embellishments, or elaborations. Hofinger urged educators to be less concerned with precise formulations and more concerned with understanding Christian doctrine in relation to living. He was not arguing for an experiential mode of education in the sense of focusing on the interpretation and reconstruction of one's present experience. He was particularly concerned with what central messages and doctrine were taught and when and how. He thought it important that people learn from the Bible, liturgy, and doctrine in order to come to some understanding of their religious meaning and their usefulness in daily life.[17] This, he thought, needed to be done in ways appropriate to the age of persons and through the catechetical methods most effective in helping persons grasp the religious meaning of the traditional content.

Cultural Influences

Several cultural influences impacted the rise of tradition-based Christian education in the United States. First, on the frontier the newness of so much of life called for many forms of adaptation and change. The Sunday school movement represented an effort to preserve the Christian heritage and values in the face of pressures for rapid change in so many areas of life.

Second, the 1930s marked the beginning of considerable disillusionment in the Western world with human "progress." Two world wars, a depression, and the mass extermination of Jews in a Christian country raised again the question of the goodness of human nature and answered in the negative. No longer could persons reflect great optimism about human nature, about human persons' building the Kingdom of God on earth, or about God's being revealed largely through humanity. H. Shelton Smith was particularly articulate about the impact of the changing-world situation. He recognized that the era of the 1940s had more pressures and crises than the preceding period of economic, social, and political advancement.[18] He thought the changing situation raised some basic questions about liberalism.

Third, new theological reflections were emerging on this historical-cultural landscape. Karl Barth was raising radical questions about the value of human achivement and about natural theology. Neo-orthodoxy was being born. Its increasing influence called experiential education into question by challenging its overemphasis on the goodness of human nature and on the immanence of God in human experience. Such leaders as H. Shelton Smith were critiquing progressive religious education sharply and seeking new approaches that would be more compatible with neo-orthodox theology. These new approaches were discussed above as one of the twentieth-century shapes of education on the side of tradition. The impact of these neo-orthodox theologians was encouragement for a turning away from the authority of human experience and a turning toward biblical authority. The impact was also a renewed emphasis on Christ and on the distinctive nature of the Christian faith and life. Under the influence of neo-orthodoxy and the emerging thought of the time, a new, more confessional era had begun.

Historical Influences Within Educational Theory

Historically, tradition-based education has almost always been the dominant cultural form. But this does not mean that it was unaffected by emerging thought patterns. In fact, tradition-based education was gaining considerably in sophistication at the same time that experience-based education was emerging.

Writing at the same time as Friedrich Froebel was Johann Herbart. Both of these German men were influenced by Pestalozzi, but Herbart took this influence in some different directions. Herbart focused his attention on the cognitive aspects of psychology and education and proposed a theory of learning and instruction. He, like Pestalozzi and Froebel, was concerned with developmental theory, but he focused on deductive rather than inductive methods of education. He outlined steps in the instructional process, and these, though systematized further by later persons, guided educators for many years.[19] As adapted by later students, these pedagogical steps were: preparation, presentation, comparison (association), generalization (systematization), and application. Teaching that followed this progression was understood to be in line with the most natural flow of students' learning. Herbart's instructional theory was very influential on both the public schools and on the curriculum and methods of the Sunday school at the turn of the century in this country. Kendig Cully notes that this influence persisted longer in the fundamentalist circles than in others.[20]

At the same time that Herbart's influence was flourishing, the Sunday school movement was exerting a major influence on the education forms in this country. As noted above, this movement was particularly impacting the churches with its tradition-based education. The largely independent lay movement was taken over by the churches in the middle years of the nineteenth century, and with the movement came its didactic methods, its focus on biblical subject matter, and its goals of inculcating persons into the Christian faith and tradition.

One other historical root of tradition-oriented education should be noted. This was a particular form of the catechetical model prominent in many churches since the Reformation. Catechesis, or oral instruction, is as old as the church itself and in the Roman Catholic Church refers to the full Christian education or nurture process. The catechetical model referred to here arose with the advent of the printing press and with the emergence of formal catechisms, or books that present Christian doctrine in question-and-answer form. This form of instruction had been formalized by Martin Luther in 1529 when he wrote the *Small Catechism* and the *Large Catechism*. These provided a resource to churches and families for teaching the fundamental tenets of the Christian faith. This method of instruction became widespread and was dominant in some churches as the twentieth century began, particularly in the Roman Catholic, Lutheran, Presbyterian, and Anglican churches. This method gave attention to the instruction of traditional subject matter and was built on the assumption that there are fundamental principles to be conveyed to each new generation.

Tradition and Experience Emphases in Tension

At no time were experience-based and tradition-based education more clearly in opposition than in the 1930s and 40s. The differences between these perspectives were highlighted in several ways. For example, in 1938 the Federal Council of Churches made an official statement that emphasized the role of transmitting the Christian tradition in Christian education. Two years later the official statement of the International Council of Religious Education placed emphasis on the reinterpretation and enrichment of experience.

In 1922 the International Council of Religious Education had produced the Bower Report, which described religious education as centered on life situations. The biblical tradition was seen as a source for guiding one's response to these life situations. In 1944 the focus of the council was changed to Christian education, and its new statement emphasized gospel-centeredness and the educational role of the churches. Paul Vieth's report arising from this council described the discipline in this way: "Christian education is the process by which persons are confronted with and controlled by the Christian gospel."[21]

The Elliott-Smith Debate

One of the most memorable debates between the experiential and traditional emphases took place in print as Harrison Elliott (representing the progressive religious education perspective) and H. Shelton Smith (representing a neo-orthodox theological perspective) articulated their views of Christian education. The arguments of these two men were far more complex than will be presented here, but some of their dominant educational assumptions will be described as these impinge on the assumed experience-tradition duality.

In *Can Religious Education Be Christian?* Harrison Elliott was trying to defend the possibility that progressive religious education can, indeed, be Christian. Writing against the background of the debate between progressive religious education and neo-orthodoxy, he set as his task to resolve some of the issues of that debate, exploring the presuppositions on both sides.

At least four of Elliott's assumptions about religious education reflect his biases toward experiential education forms.

1. Education has a role of not just passing on adult beliefs and practices but of being reconstructive, i.e., lifting life above current standards and accomplishments. This includes helping persons reconstruct the life they participate in, the inner church life, and the church's corporate action in the world.[22] In short, religious education should involve both efforts toward bringing in the Kingdom and criticisms of those efforts. Educational strategies growing out of this are social, experience-centered, inclusive across races, classes, and generations, and active in actual situations.[23]

2. Education should not be individualistic in focus, but corporate, i.e., centered on corporate goals. This is what Elliott means by a "social strategy" of education.[24]

3. Education should focus on both intellect and emotion.[25]

4. Biblical studies should be approached, not with preconceived answers, but with human issues in mind.

H. Shelton Smith represents much more bias toward tradition-based education. In *Faith and Nurture* he explored the meaning of Christian nurture in the context of faith. He appealed to what he understood to be traditional Christian faith as it was being called freshly to our attention by neo-orthodoxy. He appealed throughout to emphases that he found in the neo-orthodox movement. Basically, he was critiquing progressive, or liberal, religious education from the standpoint of traditional Christian belief. His thrust was far more in the direction of critique than of redefinition, though he was attempting to lay some groundwork for the redefining task.

Smith was trying to put forth the directions for the critique and reconstruction of Christian nurture. He pointed to some directions but did not spell them out. That work would need to follow. Below are some of the educational assumptions to which he pointed and considered to be of importance in any reformulation of religous education or Christian nurture.

1. Education is not the answer to complex social problems or to salvation or self-help.[26]

2. The focal point of curriculum should not be social relations.[27]

3. Religious education should be based on the conviction of the revelation in Jesus Christ and on the theory of human value derived from God.[28]

4. Religious education must live in the tension between the present church and the Kingdom of God. It must actively nurture in the faith but recognize the far greater fullness of the coming Kingdom.[29]

5. Christian nurture derives from Christian doctrine, which is radically different from progressive democratic education. Smith believed that Dewey's emphasis on democratic education and on religion was in conflict with Christian faith.[30]

The Debate Continues

The discussion among persons at these poles of opinion is not so clear-cut as it once was, but it is by no means dead. Obvious traces of the progressive point of view are evidenced in the writings of Ross Snyder, Paul Irwin, and others. Likewise, the emphases of James Smart, James Michael Lee, and others are more in tune with Smith's tradition-based point of view. Grouping these people together poses dangers of oversimplification, so one must hastily add that the similarity within each group breaks down when these persons are compared on grounds other than their basic orientation to historical tradition and to contemporary experience.

Shapes of Education in Contemporary Practice

The issues discussed here are hardly revelant to the practice of Christian religious education if they are not issues, also, in the educational practice of the churches. The polarization between historical tradition and contemporary experience is, in fact, prominent in the life of faith communities. It emerges in many forms, but four questions that particularly reflect this polarization will be considered here.

1. Are our children learning the Bible, or do they just play in their educational activities? This is a question very familiar to Christian educators, even in those churches where the Bible is not understood to be the sole source of God's revelation, the sole authority for Christian faith. Underlying this question is the assumption that the focus of Christian religious education is to be the transmission of the biblical content and that other activities may distract from this central goal.

2. Are our people learning the essentials of the Christian faith and life, or do we simply get together for social experiences? This kind of question surfaces in many faith communities, including those churches that are not doctrinal and that do not have a clearly articulated set of essential beliefs and practices. This question comes out of two primary assumptions: (a) that there are certain Christian beliefs and practices to be taught and learned and (b) that Christian faith is transmitted, not through social experience, but through telling people what to do and their doing it.

3. Why can't we do away with archaic and oppressive educational settings and forms and let the church community educate through its corporate life? The assumptions behind this particular question are: (a) that direct, purposeful, and communal experience takes the place of systematic study and

(b) that the church school setting itself is limited to certain forms of instruction that are fundamentally incompatible with intrinsically rewarding and corporate experience. In other words, the Sunday school or study settings are seen to be essentially irrelevant to the education process. The assumption is that education can be done much more effectively through other means.

4. Why can't the education of the church be relevant to the issues that people face in their life rather than focusing so much on irrelevant theological concepts? This question leads into the perennial argument for starting with the life experience of the learners and communicating only what is relevant to those life experiences. Assumed in this question is the idea that the biblical and historical traditions should only be studied when clearly and directly relevant to some aspect of the learners' life experience. Hence, the history of the church would not necessarily be taught to older children or to early teens because of unclear linkage with the immediate life concerns of these young people.

Any of these four questions suggests an either/or dichotomy. The first two suggest that education needs to be transmissive of a certain body of historical and unchanging tradition. The last two suggest that education needs to be built more on the contemporary experiences of persons, both the experiences of the faith community and the experiences of the people in their everyday life.

One would be naïve to not recognize the values of these shifts in emphases at particular times and places. Persons arguing for one side or the other of the polarity are often speaking from their own skewed experience with the other pole. This does not warrant, however, a resignation to a swinging-pendulum theory that accepts the inevitability of alternating educational emphases between the poles of historical tradition and contemporary experience. We will now turn to a brief look at some of the persons who have attempted to push beyond this dichotomy in educational theory and practice.

Movements Toward Synthesis

Concern over this dichotomy is not new. Many educators have attempted to avoid the either/or choice between education for continuity with historical tradition and education for change based on present experience.

John Dewey

We began with John Dewey's cry against such dualism, so we can appropriately begin now with his own attempt to resolve the dilemma. Though Dewey was a major catalyst in experiential education, he attempted in his later years to escape the tradition/experience dichotomy by articulating a philosophy of experience. He thought that if the idea of experience were properly conceived adequate account would be taken of the historical tradition in the educational process.[31] Dewey saw this as possible if adequate attention were given to the quality of experience. By quality he meant both the immediate agreeableness of the experience and its effect on the future.[32]

Dewey elaborated his theory of experience by stating two principal criteria for assessing the value of any experience. The first criterion was whether or not the experience leads to growth. Dewey appealed here to the principle of continuity, asserting "that every experience both takes up something from those which have gone before and modifies in some way the quality of those which come after."[33] The continuity of experience is inevitable because present experience is always linked to the past and future. The important question is whether present experiences contribute to the continuation of growth, e.g., by increasing options or by inspiring openness to new experiences. He hoped that the work of educators would be fruitful by helping persons to grow and by changing external conditions to be more conducive to further growth. Education, then, was viewed by Dewey as a continuing process of reconstructing experience, informed always by what has gone before and what will come after.

The second criterion for Dewey was whether the experience involves interaction between objective and internal conditions.[34] By this he meant interaction between the objective knowledge of the past and social structures and the internal needs and desires of the students. Dewey was recognizing the importance of persons' gaining knowledge and learning to organize facts and ideas.[35] He was also recognizing the importance of these facts and ideas' being connected to persons' own experiences. Further, Dewey was suggesting that education needs to be an interactive and social experience in which both students and teachers are part. In other words the learning situation should not be dominated by either students or teachers but should be a situation of "mutual accommodation and adaptation."[36] All this would suggest that education needs to be informed by both developmental theory (concerned primarily with internal conditions of students) and learning and instructional theory (concerned primarily with external conditions of experience).

John Dewey did indeed go far in his later writing in conceiving of education beyond dichotomies of either/or. Thomas Groome has recently bemoaned, however, that Dewey's "call for a synthesis . . . has continued to be more honored in the breach than in the observance."[37] Groome thinks this may be due to Dewey's failure to "spell out a teaching methodology that would bring about such balance between the disciplines of knowledge and present experience."[38]

Contemporary Syntheses

In recent years educational theories and methods have emerged that are conceived to bring together these two poles in Christian education. Three dominant forms of theory have emerged, each offering its own unique mode of synthesis.

Socialization Theories

Ellis Nelson and John Westerhoff have aroused considerable interest in their socialization models of education. They have stirred freshly a sense of the value of historical tradition in Christian education and of the dynamic and communal process of handing it on. In so doing, they have given attention to the unity of historical tradition and of contemporary experience. This is illustrated nowhere better than in Westerhoff's quote of Nelson. "Faith is communicated by a community of believers and the meaning of faith is developed by its members out of their history, by their interaction with each other, and in relation to the events that take place in their lives."[39]

Westerhoff's emphasis has been on the communal context of Christian education, recognizing the need to break out of narrow schooling/instructional models and to "focus our attention on the radical nature and character of the church as a faith community."[40] He and Gwen Neville call attention to the role of community life in Christian education, including the rites, the interactions, the actions in the world, and the liturgy.[41] Westerhoff suggests that Christians are called to be a community of change, to be in the world but not of the world. At the same time, however, he holds up the shared memory and vision of the Christian community and urges the transmission of the Christian story as our story.

Nelson has focused even more directly on the nature of the union between historical tradition and contemporary experience. He suggests that the connector between the past and present is tradition.[42] He sees tradition as the very process of transmission. Biblical tradition, for example, includes two elements: "the tradition that is handed down and the experience that individuals and groups have as they live, modify, and pass on the tradition."[43] Thus tradition is continually formed and reformed.[44] It is not just something from the past but is a dynamic part of the community in the present. This calls for more intentional focus on tradition and its process. For Nelson, "Both the conservation and the creative adaptation of tradition are bound up in the dynamic process of passing it on. Therefore, we must be much clearer about the way in which we use events that are happening—and events we cause to happen—as the key to our communication of faith."[45] In all this, Nelson's attention is on past and present rather than on future.

Nelson contributes another important element to the tradition and experience discussions. He gives particular attention to the question of revelation, the unique experience of God that makes persons more aware of their tradition and enables them also to critique and change that tradition. This is the kind of experience that helps persons transcend themselves and their culture. It is the experience that "breaks through the culture and gives the receiver a meaningful word about himself and the human situation for which he must take responsibility."[46] Nelson is concerned that Christian education opens persons in some way to revelation as well as transmits tradition so that the latter can inform and form their experience.[47]

Dialogical Theories

A more dialogical point of view has emerged in education, partially in reaction against the socialization model, particularly against the danger in that model of romanticizing a community's perpetuating itself uncritically with all its inadequacies.[48] In the dialogical point of view, education is conceived as a process of opening the present to both the past and the future.

Thomas Groome has put forth a dialogical model of Christian education that he calls critical reflection on shared praxis.[49] Groome sees the starting point of education as the present experience and action of persons. Persons are to reflect on this experience in light of the community's tradition, or story, and its vision of the Kingdom of God. The community's story and vision serve as a critique of persons' present experience and as a guide to future action. At the same time the present experience of persons serves as a critique of the community's tradition and may lead to its revision. In his model Groome takes seriously the prophetic role of Christian education in opening the way for the Christian community to be transformed.

Another theory that could be called dialogical has been suggested by Mary Boys. Boys speaks of religious education as "making accessible" both tradition and transformation.[50] She emphasizes the inseparability of these dynamics and the importance of religious education's opening access to the past and to the critical interpretation and reconstruction of that past in the present.

Transcending Theories

Still another category of theory that rises valiantly above the stark dichotomizing of historical tradition and contemporary experience is what I am calling the transcending theories. Philip Phenix has used this word *transcendence* as a way of interpreting education.[51] Interestingly, the emphasis on the relationship between education and transcendence has appeared less in the religious education literature per se and more in the literature of the philosophy of education. Two brilliant presentations of this emphasis are found in Dwayne Huebner and in Bernard Meland.

Huebner calls strongly for a critique of educators' preoccupation with objectives and learning. He recognizes education's indebtedness to modern technology and the social sciences for these concepts, but he calls attention instead to what he sees as the often-neglected aspect of education, the "moment of vision."

> Neither of the categories—objectives nor learning—provides guidelines for the third essential ingredient of the education environment: the moment of vision. The student, either by his own understanding or that of others, must be able to envision his own projected potentiality for being as it exists in the past-present-future. This is the uniquely human quality of the environment and requires the presence of human wisdom. This is the unique function of the teacher, the human aspect of that specific educational environment, who shares the rhythms of continuity and change, of necessity and freedom, with his students.[52]

For Huebner, this possibility of self-transcendence is itself a dimension of the education process that transcends the limits placed by educators who are solely concerned with objectives and learning.

Another voice that calls out for this possibility of self-transcendence is Bernard Meland. Meland's central concern is with what he calls appreciative consciousness, which is a creative openness to the values of the past and to the possibilities of the present and future. Meland describes appreciative consciousness as "the creative response in man which relates him seriously to the creative passage and to the emerging events which ensue. . . . [I]t is concerned simultaneously with past qualitative attainment, and the mystery and possibility of the new."[53] Meland holds forth an ideal of human spirit in which the appreciative consciousness is nurtured both through critical inquiry and through affective imagination.[54] For him the critical and imaginative, the scientific and artistic, need to be integrated in the human spirit if persons are to be responsive in the way that is possible and ideal for human beings.

Maria Harris suggests that transcendence in education moves beyond the dichotomizing of tradition and transformation by making us aware that the tradition is existent in the lives of the people and is continually being recreated. She understands religious education as the facilitation of this dynamic relationship between tradition and transformation through word, sacrament, and prophecy.[55] Harris does not, however, elaborate her understanding of transcendence. That task would lie ahead.

Dualities in Transition

With all these new developments in education theory, the tendency to dichotomize continuity and change persists in educational practice. Perhaps we have not sufficiently mined the theories for educational implications. Perhaps, with Letty Russell, we must recognize "the gap between such a synthesis in theory and in educational practice."[56] Creating a synthesis in practice may be more difficult than in theory, and some of the practical dimensions of the problem may not even have been addressed yet. Perhaps, more has been accomplished in stating the problem than in suggesting resolution.

The description of the continuity/change dualism leaves many unanswered questions. Even in the impressive collection of essays in *Tradition and Transformation in Religious Education,* the problem is primarily stated in terms of the past/present tension with little attention given to the relationship of either to future. Even more important, the suggested educational theories and methods are left still in skeletal form. The issue has certainly been highlighted and brought into clearer focus, but the insights in these essays have yet to be fully developed. Huebner has expressed a similar concern in his concluding response to these essays: that the issue of tradition and transformation has yet to be considered in the context of nonacademic religious communities and in the actions and questions of educational practitioners.[57] Huebner also calls for attention to be given to the historical precedents of educational language in hopes that a more public language might emerge for religious education.[58] This would be a language in line with the questions and thinking of both clergy and laity, educators and educatees, adults and children.

The challenge before us, then, is the assimilation of insights from all these people who have spoken and an attempt toward fresh insight and direction. Wide agreement seems to exist in Christian religious education that attention needs to be given to both historical tradition and contemporary experience, to both continuity and change. What seems to be lacking is the assimilation of insights from the several directions and the reformulation of educational theory and practice.

Conclusions for Education Theory and Practice

The visions presented here are rich in possibilities for Christian religious education. Some conclusions may be drawn from these to inform the traditioning model being developed here. Indeed, the conclusions form some of the basic assumptions underlying that theory.

1. The tendency to dichotomize tradition and experience is real and is not easily overcome by pleas to rise above it. The sheer number of educational theorists who have given attention to the problem directly or indirectly testifies to that fact. The problem has been with us for centuries and does not promise to retreat quickly or quietly.

2. The tradition/experience dichotomy is essentially a false one, in that understanding either side deeply leads a person into the other. John Dewey's rich understanding of experience led him in his later years to conceive of education as having a significant role in communicating the historical tradition and the disciplines of knowledge. These were conceived as important factors in enabling persons to understand and to organize their present experiences. Similarly, Ellis Nelson has probed deeply into the meaning of tradition, particularly the biblical tradition. He has concluded that tradition itself is dynamic, including both what is handed down from the past and the experience of persons in the present as they hand it down and live it. Further, both Nelson and Boys have recognized the inevitable impact of historical tradition in forming and interpreting our present experience.

3. Past, present, and future are all vital to the subject matter of Christian religious education. We need to look to the past because it has formed us. We need, as Nelson urges, to enable our past to inform us as well.[59] It is this past that provides us with knowledge that can help us discover our roots and interpret and organize our present experience. It is this past, also, that confronts us from outside our immediate experience so that we may learn who we are. As Boys suggests, "It is not the hearer who interprets the parable, but the parable which interprets the hearer."[60]

We need, also, to look to the present, the contemporary life of the faith community that carries and modifies the tradition in its very living of it. Not only that, but the present includes the experience of contemporary culture that affects the life of the faith community and is affected by it. We need to envision education that responds to the heartbeat of that cultural context, as did Coe and Dewey and the leaders of the Sunday school movement. The present must also include the contemporary experience of God, a recognition of God's continuing involvement in the world and an openness to God's continuing revelation. Meland's concern with appreciative consciousness and Nelson's interest in revelation call attention to this vital aspect of present experience.

Finally, we need to look to the future, both in terms of our hopes and vision of God's future and in terms of our anticipation of the problems and issues that will be facing our globe. Thomas Groome's model of Christian religious education as shared praxis is very similar to those earlier progressive models of Bower and Elliott, but he adds the very important focus on eschatology, on the Christian vision of the Kingdom of God. Dewey has emphasized another aspect of the future focus in education, i.e., the anticipated issues of the future (such as the anticipated necessity for more radical energy conservation or for new forms of living in human community). Education, then, should be designed around the past and present experiences of persons and cultures and also around anticipated crises, questions, and decisions. These emphases on the future can perhaps help us overcome our preoccupation with the immediate relevance of education and our often-narrow focus on one particular community or social context for our education efforts.

4. Christian religious education must tap the resources of both critical reflection and imagination. These dual themes are particularly emphasized by Bernard Meland, Mary Boys, and Maria Harris as movements that enrich one another. Christian education must be conceived as critical reflection, bringing to bear all the knowledge of the past and present and critically evaluating and drawing from it. Christian education

must also stir imagination, jolting persons out of the expected and routine into participation in mystery.

5. Christian religious education must be a social and interactive experience in which the entire faith community is involved and in which both teachers and students are dynamic participants. This would suggest that education is informed both by developmental theory (concerned primarily with internal conditions of the participants) and learning and instructional theories (concerned primarily with teaching methods and external conditions such as the physical environment).

6. The assumptions underlying educational theory and practice must be reexamined in every era. H. Shelton Smith and Harrison Elliott made valuable contributions in performing that kind of analysis of their viewpoints in the 1940s. We must look behind any model to the educational, theological, philosophical, and social-psychological assumptions on which it is built. This is the way we can critique and revise, e.g., we can perceive in retrospect some of the assumptions of our predecessors, such as George Albert Coe and leaders of the Sunday school movement. In recognizing the valuable social function of Coe's model of progressive religious education in an emerging technological-democratic society and of the function of the Sunday school movement on the frontier, we must remember the limitations of both those models to the social, political, and theological assumptions of their particular social contexts. In drawing from those models we must recognize the ways in which the present context is different, and we must respond to the particular needs and issues of a new era, always questioning our own assumptions as well.

7. Christian religious education can be a visionary discipline, seeking faith visions in the historical Christian tradition, contemporary experience, and future hope. Much of tradition-oriented education has sought to apply the knowledge of tradition to particular problems of contemporary life. Much of experience-based education has sought to understand contemporary problems and reach into the historical tradition

and contemporary knowledge for answers. Both are thereby limited to problems and often to a bias that the answers are usually in the historical tradition. What might emerge if we sought faith visions in the past, present, and future of the Christian story, rather than static problems and solutions?

2 FOUNDATIONS FOR A MODEL

Whatever else can be said, Christian religious education always takes place in a community of faith and involves persons as participants in the educational process. Understanding the nature of that community and those persons becomes extremely important to the design of a new model of education.

Reexamining these foundations of Christian religious education will certainly involve upsetting some applecarts. What is hoped is that such a turning over will lead to careful examination of the apples, including some that have been lost on the bottom and also a careful examination of the upturned carts. The ideas and practices that have been included in our models of Christian community and of human persons must not be lost but must be freshly examined. The hope here is that this examination will lead to the construction of new carts that may be more adequate for carrying the apple riches of the past and those yet to be harvested. The hope is, too, that these models of Christian community and of human persons will provide more adequate foundations for a model of Christian religious education, one that avoids the dichotomizing so characteristic of many of its predecessors.

We will examine the nature of the traditioning community in chapter 3 and the nature of the person in process in chapter 4.

The Traditioning Community

We begin this examination of foundations by struggling to define the nature of the Christian community and its relationship to the continuity/change question. The Christian church has often been recognized as a preserving community or as an agent of change. Many debates have taken place in the church's history over the conflict between these two points of view. No clear answer exists for resolving this tension, but let us hope that the tension never gives way to one pole or the other.

The title of this chapter suggests a choice for the continuity pole, but do not be so easily deceived. Tradition, as suggested in chapter 1, is a process of handing over God's gifts. If God had acted only in the past, then tradition would simply involve preserving the past. But if God has acted in the past, is acting now, and will act in the future, then tradition involves living in a stream of history, keeping alive the memory, participating in God's present action, and hoping for God's future.

We will here examine the nature of this traditioning community by exploring some historical images of the church, the historical nature of the Christian community, and the functions of historical tradition and of contemporary experience in that community. A perspective on the church as a traditioning community will be elaborated to take account of the rich imagery and historical nature of the Christian community and to foster the church's sense of its own past, present, and future.

Historical Images of the Church

The church cannot easily be explained in one word or phrase. It is a community defined by many images and shapes. Both in the Bible and in the history of the church these images have existed together in different combinations with different emphases.

The biblical word usually translated as "church" is *ekklesia,* which refers to the "called out ones," or the assembled people of God who are heirs to God's promises of the Kingdom. This word can refer to a particular local congregation or to the universal church. Whichever reference is made, the *ekklesia* is the people of God who are summoned or called out, who gather, and who look toward God's future kingdom.

A related term is *laos,* which translates as "people of God" and which is often used to refer to God's chosen people.[1] The English word *laity* obscures the full meaning of *laos* and has come to refer to persons who are not clergy rather than to persons who are part of the people of God. The term *laos* suggests a relatedness to God and a participation in God's creation.

Two other words appear frequently in the New Testament description of church. These are *koinonia* and *diakonia*. The koinonia is a fellowship or sharing community bound together by common relationship to God. This is a group that shares together in the gifts of God and with each other in real, concrete ways (e.g., the sharing of possessions in the early church). Referring to the understanding of tradition put forth in chapter 1, this is the community that has been given the Tradition and that is called to pass it on. The community shares together in that gift and in that task.

The *diakonia* are the serving people, the people who are called to minister to each other and who are sent out into the world to serve. In the New Testament this word sometimes refers to certain leaders in the community who had particular roles in serving the people. The word was also used to refer to the entire serving community. Everyone was called to serve both within the community itself and outside of it. They were called to serve the physical and spiritual needs of persons all around them.

Two other dimensions are associated in the New Testament with the life of the Christian community: the kerygma and the *leitourgia*. The kerygma was understood to be the announcement of the good news of Jesus Christ, or the proclamation of the gospel message. It included both the message itself and the proclaiming of it. The early Christian community was a proclaiming community with a message to share. The hymn "We've a Story to Tell to the Nations" captures some of that burning sense of a message to tell and a desire to tell it.

The *leitourgia* was understood to be the liturgical life of the community. One finds in many accounts of the early church a reference to worship, to the hymns, prayers, and sacraments of the community. The Christian community, then, is the people of God called out, the people who are engaged in sharing, serving, proclaiming, and worshiping.

In short, the imagery of the New Testament church is rich, and when one considers this imagery in light of the Old Testament imagery of the people of God the shapes become richer. This is the community that is sought by God, even when undeserving. This is the community that is created, delivered, guided, commanded, chastised, and promised by God. This is the community of the covenant.

The history of the church builds on this early history and is marked by similar richness of images. Avery Dulles reviews five major models of the church functioning in Protestantism and Roman Catholicism. Dulles notes the coexistence of these models in various combinations and the tendency in the history of the church to swing from one emphasis or one combination of emphases to another. The models he describes are: the church as institution, as mystical communion, as sacrament, as herald, and as servant. Each of these models catches up a variety of biblical and historical images of the church and has functioned in various parts of the church. Dulles sees this variety of models as necessary and valuable.

The peculiarity of models, as contrasted with aspects, is that we cannot integrate them into a single synthetic vision on the level of articulate, categorical thought. In order to do justice to the various aspects of the church, as a complex reality, we must work simultaneously with different models.[2]

Again, the richness of ideas about the church is evident.

The problem that this plethora of images leaves for the church is clear. What is the church? How can you state your answer in one easy sentence that everyone can learn and understand? You cannot, and that is the problem. Images are abundant, and no one image is without some mystery. Paul Minear reviews approximately one hundred New Testament images of the church and notes that no writer has seemed inclined "to reduce the profusion to order, to weave the various strands into a single tapestry, or to arrange the kinds of figurative language into a neat pattern."[3] Moreover, Minear recognizes the value of such a profusion of images.

The purpose of every comparison is to point beyond itself. The greater the number of comparisons, the greater the number of pointers. When so many separate pointers impel our eyes to look in one direction, our comprehension of the magnitude of what lies in that direction is enhanced.[4]

A similar point of view is held by Avery Dulles, who emphasizes the mystery of the church. The mystery is approached through analogies in the form of various models, but it can never be summarized by any one model or even by one combination. For Dulles, the term mystery "implies that the Church is not fully intelligible to the finite mind of man, and that the reason for this lack of intelligibility is not the poverty but the richness of the Church itself."[5]

And so we are left with profusion, but we are also left with some ambiguity. Phrases like body of Christ, people of God, and community of the Spirit are very suggestive. They are rich in pictures and ideas but are not easy to grasp. Every time you turn the phrases a different way you get a new elusiveness, and one could say that in some sense they escape definition. This accounts for disagreements about the nature and mission of the church. One faction is thoroughly convinced that the church exists to serve the physical needs of the world (God's creation). Another faction is equally convinced that the church exists to provide a centering place of worship for the Christian community. Still another faction believes that the church is only the church when it is preaching the gospel to those who need to hear it and calling persons to repentance and belief. These disagreements are very real and have led to schisms and divisions throughout the church's history.

To say that the Christian community escapes definition is not to say, however, that we cannot say anything about it. Quite to the contrary, we can never say enough about it. It will always be larger than our words. With that recognition we launch into a study of the historical nature of the Christian community. To talk about education for continuity and change is to assume that the Christian communty in which education takes place is a historical community with a past, a present, and a future. The understanding of that community will influence the model of education developed here.

Historical Nature of the Christian Community

The Christian community does indeed have a past, present, and future, but these do not exist as three isolated bits of time. Neither do they meld together so as to lose their distinctiveness. The past affects and becomes part of the present and future, but it is still past. Likewise the future has helped form the past and is now forming the present, but the future is still future. It is not yet. The church lives in the midst of a living stream of tradition deeply influenced by this past and future and by its present life. What is the nature of this church then?

Related to God

The Christian church is the community called by God, the *ekklesia* (the called out and gathered community) or the *laos* (the people of God). This is the community that experiences God's revelation and follows.

In this relationship with God, mystery does indeed exist, but this relationship is not an abstraction. It finds expression in real and concrete ways. As persons function in a prophetic role, the personal experience of God is transformed into acts in the social order: cries for social justice, acts of mercy, work toward social reform. Witness Moses and the prophets whose personal experience of God transformed them and through them the social order. As persons function in a priestly role, the personal or community experience of God is transformed into ritual that then becomes available to be shared more widely in the form of psalms, hymns, and sacramental acts.

Related to the World

The Christian church exists in the world and for the world. It is called out from the world (*ekklesia*), sent back into the world (*diakonia*), and formed by it so that the rituals, the music, the self-understanding, and the work of that community are influenced by its social-historical context.

The church stands in relationship to the world of past, present, and future. The influence of present events and cultural practices on the life of the church is inevitable. The church often responds directly to these events and practices, and its own work and life reflect these. In the last chapter we saw how the Industrial Revolution and optimistic spirit in the late nineteenth-century United States influenced the advent of liberal theology and progressive religious education. Likewise, we saw how the two world wars and depression in the twentieth century influenced the advent of neo-orthodoxy and neo-orthodox formulations of Christian education.

We must also recognize that what is expected in the future or what has occurred in the past influences the church as much as does the present world situation. For example, the fear of world war, mounting problems of hunger, or economic disaster influences the church's understanding of its mission so that persons who previously thought the church had no role in politics begin to affirm the need for the church to take an active political role. Similarly, certain worship practices (e.g., the use of icons or candles) may be associated with certain past experiences of a religious group and may be rejected by that group as inappropriate to Christian worship. The same practices may seem quite appropriate to another religious group with another history. For the first group, the rejection of these practices may be the way they reject aspects of their past experience (e.g., with other religious groups) that they consider non-Christian or destructive of the most important Christian values. For the second group, the practices may seem quite compatible with their own past experiences and understanding of Christian values.

The church's relationship to the world has always been a dialectical one. The church stands apart from the world and yet in it. It stands over against the world and in ministry to this world, and yet the people of the church are themselves living in the world and formed by its influences. Hence, many Christian festivals have adopted practices that were part of various cultural groups at a particular time and place. At the same time the Christian church has often rejected such practices. It has critiqued the culture and defined itself in opposition to certain cultural influences. It has been engaged throughout its history in acts of both cultural assimilation and social change.

Bearer of Tradition

Tradition itself is historical in that it is a process taking place in history. As pointed out in chapter 1, the Christian community is gifted by God with Tradition and is also given the responsibility for passing this on through the process of tradition.

The church's role in passing on tradition is reflected in its sacramental life in which the meaning of the sacrament is passed on in the ritual acts. Whether the sacrament of the eucharist is viewed as re-presentation of Christ's body and blood or as a memorial of Christ's death for humanity, the community is recognizing in that sacrament the gift of God freely given in Christ and passed on through the sacramental acts of the Christian church.

The church's role in passing on tradition is also reflected in its preaching and teaching. These functions of proclaiming and imparting the community's wisdom have been important dimensions of the church since its inception. The preaching and teaching have not been seen as empty demonstrations of verbal skill or as formalities separate from the life of the community. Rather, the preaching and teaching have been understood to be at the heart of the Christian community as it engages in passing on the gifts of God. For example, the Apostles' Creed was taught in the early church to persons preparing for baptism. These persons then said that creed as part of the ritual. The creed was not understood simply as human teaching, and learning the creed was not understood as just one more task to accomplish. The creed was itself a symbol of the gifts of God (Tradition) given first to the apostles and by them to others and by them to others and so forth. The idea that the creed actually derived from the twelve apostles faded by the end of the Middle Ages (and far earlier among the best minds), but still the creed symbolically represented apostolic faith that is delivered and received at baptism.[6] What is passed on, then, is the gifts of God delivered through Christ to the world and continually delivered through persons to each other. Teaching, then, is a means of passing on the tradition, of continuing the handing over of the gifts of God. What would happen if we took our preaching and teaching this seriously?

Living Toward the Future

The Christian community is not only related to God and the world as the bearer of tradition but is also a community that lives toward the future. It is a community of promise and of mission. The promise of the Kingdom of God was the guiding image for the New Testament church, and this image has been renewed in various forms throughout Christian history. The centrality of the Kingdom of God in Jesus' own preaching and teaching suggests that we cannot carry on the work of Christ without taking seriously the Kingdom, which is both present and future. The theologians of hope and liberation theologians are today calling us to take very seriously what this means for the Christian community.

Jürgen Moltmann in particular has recognized the significance of the Christian community as a community of promise. He emphasizes the idea that God is revealed in the event of promise.[7] He also emphasizes that the origin of Christian hope is in God's promises.

A community of promise must also be a community of mission. The church is the community called to proclaim God's promise and to embody it in acts of faith. This is the community called to continue the work of Christ, which itself embodied the promise and pointed toward the future.

All this description of the historical nature of the church forces us to recognize that the life of this community is indeed historical. Its nature is not static, for it grows out of its past and present and future as they come together. The traditioning community is one that has form. We can describe its nature, but we must recognize that this nature is itself always subject to both continuity and change.

Functions of Historical Tradition and Contemporary Experience in the Community

If the church is historical, then what are the functions of past, present, and future in that community? In this section we will examine particularly the functions of historical tradition and contemporary experience since these have been the dual emphases through much of recent history. We have already noted that this so-called duality is inadequate because it does not take account of the breadth of meaning in the concepts of either tradition or experience. Neither does it take account of the future. It does frame a very lively and real theological argument.

When we ask what are the functions of historical tradition and contemporary experience in the community, we are really asking a question of theological method. How do we go about theologizing? We have already noted in chapter 1 that the prophets appealed to both historical tradition and their contemporary experience of God and the world as they engaged in their theological searching and reflection. In this way each came to a unique message for a particular time and place. Likewise did Jesus. Jesus' teaching was filled with references to both Jewish tradition and his own immediate experience of God and the world.

Despite this fact that both historical tradition and contemporary experience have functioned in the Judeo-Christian communities, the two have often been polarized as authorities for theological reflection. In twentieth-century theology the pendulum has swung between them with particular vigor. We will examine here how these two have functioned in various twentieth-century approaches. We will examine first the nature of the community's theological task and then the sources of authority (past, present, or future) from which that community has drawn.

The Theologizing Community

The theologizing community is the setting where historical tradition, contemporary experience, and future hope coexist and exercise their influence. What do we mean by the theologizing community? Theology is simply the studied expression of faith. John Macquarrie's definition is an elaboration of this simple one and informs our work here: "Theology may be defined as the study which, through participation in and reflection upon a religious faith, seeks to express the content of this faith in the clearest and most coherent language available."[8] This suggests that the Christian community is necessarily engaged in theologizing, or forming theology, if it is to function as a community of faith. Theologizing is not abstracted from the life of that community. It involves both participation in and reflection on that community's faith, what Maurice Wiles calls a combination of faith and critical detachment.[9] It has elements of both subjectivity and objectivity.

Theology, then, is a study from within faith. This is true for both the academic theologian and the theologizing persons in the parish. John Cobb recognizes this faith orientation of the theologian: "The Christian theologian is one who believes the Christ event is the source of the deepest insight into the nature of reality."[10] This study of faith from within faith raises the question of subjectivity. Maurice Wiles recognizes this as a necessary aspect of theology.

> If there were no religious faith, there would be no theology. It would therefore be absurd to suggest that there is not or should not be a close connexion between faith and theology. Moreover it is grossly misleading to suggest that an attitude of no faith represents a desirable position of neutrality. . . . Someone who is thoroughly uninterested in political affairs is unlikely to make a good political scientist. But nor on the other hand is the most passionately committed party politician.[11]

Herein lies the dilemma. What is the appropriate degree of subjectivity? After all, the theological task of the faith community is hopefully tied to deep dedication and commitment on the part of the people.

Theology also requires reflection on faith, which involves some stepping-back, or objectivity, a seeking after clarity and coherence and an application of reason to faith. Wiles insists this means not that the theologian should have less faith, but that the theologian's faith should be accompanied by a "capacity for detachment."[12] This idea suggests that the subjectivity and objectivity of the theological task are not mutually exclusive but can complement each other.

This does not mean that the subjectivity and objectivity will not stand in tension. What it does mean is that the tension can be fruitful, leading to a deepening and transforming of faith. This, in itself, may be threatening, for it suggests that faith cannot be pinned down to a certain set of unchanging beliefs or assumptions. John Macquarrie recognizes this as he reflects on the double nature of theology.

> Theology is therefore at once the self-expression and the self-criticism of the community's beliefs. It follows that theology is not a static science. There is development of doctrine as beliefs and their implications come to be better understood or as older formulations are revised in light of new knowledge and criticism. The task of theology is never finished and there cannot be any final theology.[13]

To recognize this dynamic nature of theology is to recognize that the traditioning community does not have a theology so much as it theologizes. That community is continually forming and reforming its faith expressions in light of its past, present, and future.

All this leads to the conclusion that all Christians are theologians because we all stand within faith. We have certain faith assumptions that need to be clarified, broadened, deepened, or transformed. This does not mean that we do not need academic theologians or specialists, but the church in its teaching ministry has a role in helping all its people in their theologizing, in their living of faith and in their reflections on that faith. Faith here is understood as an active way of being that includes all dimensions of personhood: believing, feeling, willing, and acting.[14] The study of faith, then, will involve the study of beliefs, attitudes, commitments, and practices. No one dimension can be singled out to the exclusion of the others.

Sources of Authority

How does the community proceed with its theological reflection? What are its sources of authority? We are concerned here with the life and practice of the church, and we can quickly see that a tension has existed in the church between applied and empirical methods of theologizing. The former is often based on historical tradition and draws its authority from there. The latter is based primarily on present experience from which it draws its authority. Variations exist within each of these two approaches, of course, and variations exist that combine elements of both.[15] The dichotomy is here oversimplified, but the issue is a real one. The dichotomy is presented here to call attention to the tension that often exists between historical tradition and contemporary experience as authoritative in the various approaches to theology. The particular focus will be on twentieth-century approaches.

Applied Theology

Applied theology attempts to articulate some basic Christian beliefs or ideas and to apply these to present experience. When these basic beliefs and ideas are drawn from the historical tradition, as they often are, the sources of authority are taken to be primarily historical. This can take many forms. The historical doctrines of the church can be taken as norms for theological reflection, or the biblical witness can be taken as normative. In either case the community takes some aspect of the historical tradition as its starting point or source of authority.

Applied theology is sometimes called normative in that the norms are sought in the historical tradition to guide the community in its present life. The word norm can imply anything from an absolute rule to a standard or model. Thus, applied theology may refer to the application of rigid rules and principles from the past or, simply, to the search for general guiding norms in the interpretation of Scripture or church tradition. Whichever be the case, applied theology often stresses the importance of seeking answers and guidance for the church's life in the historical tradition. For Karl Barth and Emil Brunner this means that the life of the church must seek and proclaim the Word of God as revealed in Scripture. The

Scripture, mediated by the Holy Spirit, provides the guiding norm.[16] For some Roman Catholic theologians this means that the life of the church must be guided by the historical doctrines of the church.[17] In the ongoing life of the churches, conflicts arise over which of these shall be taken as normative or how they can be held together.

The distinction between these two historical emphases (Scripture and the church's tradition) has been a major issue in the history of the church at points, but John Macquarrie has recognized how inextricable they are from each other.[18] The biblical witness grows out of earlier traditions, and the church's traditions grow out of the biblical witness. To think that one can be authoritatively independent of the other is to fail to recognize the sense in which the biblical witness is a written expression of the traditional beliefs and practices of the Judeo-Christian communities and the sense in which the post–New Testament history of the church involved the continuing interpretation and reinterpretation of Scripture.

The applied approach to theology has the advantage of offering a clear referent for practical questions as well as guidelines for action that guard against pure relativism. Further, it offers a community of ideas and persons against which a person can test his or her interpretations and decisions. This makes continuity possible between past and present and guards against faddism.

On the other side, however, applied theology that appeals wholly or principally to historical tradition runs the risk of rigidity and irrelevance to the contemporary situation. Also, the question arises as to whether persons can draw solely from the past without having their perceptions colored by their present context. Gordon Kaufman points to some of the logical inconsistencies in Barth's approach to theology. Barth's push for an independent theological method is an attempt to extricate the theological norms from their cultural distortions. Kaufman points out that this is not possible. Further, there is a problem of defining just what God's final and authoritative revelation is.[19]

The Christian education models emerging out of an applied theology are deductive. An example would be the catechetical model of teaching certain beliefs or teaching the content of Scripture or historical Christian tradition with the purpose of leading students to assent to correct belief. The content of education arising from applied theology would likely stress historical or biblical sources. The modes would likely be such settings as classrooms, worship services, lecture series, and didactic Bible studies.

Empirical Theology

The empirical approach in theology is one in which persons begin with present experience as the theological data and try to express the meaning of that in their beliefs and actions. The empirical theologian is most basically concerned with discerning the truth in the human situation. Underlying this effort is the assumption that there is theological meaning revealed in life experiences, including experiences within the church.

Important to the empirical mode of theologizing is the assumption that truth indeed can be discerned in the human situation. Friedrich Schleiermacher has been both lauded and criticized for his idea that theological reflection begins with a feeling of absolute dependence and that theology is an attempt to understand and articulate this feeling. Schleiermacher believed that the very experience of absolute dependence points to God.[20] This conclusion was possible for Schleiermacher because he believed all reality to be one, so that a person's own deepest experience is related to all reality. This idea is expressed as "the doctrine of the union of the Divine Essence with human nature, both in the personality of Christ and in the common Spirit of the Church."[21] This means that Christian faith experience is united with the Divine in such a way that the study of human experience tells us something about the Divine.[22]

Also included in the empirical mode of theologizing is a

dialogue with the human sciences that takes account of and interprets the findings there. Don Browning suggests a relationship between theology and the human sciences that is dialogic. His analogical (or perspectival) approach to pastoral theology involves theology in dialogue with other perspectives on reality.[23] Likewise, Kaufman comes to what he calls a perspectival approach, which suggests that theology is one perspective for observing and interpreting the human condition.[24] This approach to theological interpretation takes account of both contemporary experience and the light that human sciences shed on that experience. It attempts, then, to give theological interpretation to those facts and to give them a deeper meaning than mere description can do. Both Kaufman and Browning are theologizing empirically in the sense of drawing truth from life experience and of utilizing insights from the human sciences.

The strengths of theologizing empirically are that the motivation for theologizing comes from human experience in the first place[25] and that the relevance of theology to the human situation is encouraged when theological formulations are derived from the human situation. Daniel Day Williams and Anton Boisen particularly stress the relating of theological concepts to human experience.[26] Liberation theologians are today emphasizing the human situation both as data and as a motivating factor for our theologizing.

The empirical approach also offers an important corrective to applied theology, which does not always acknowledge its being influenced by preconceived notions. An empirical approach to theology offers a means for making explicit the influence of the human situation and our own cultural context on our theological formulations. Allen Moore suggests that theology cannot be separated from the cultural context anyway, and similarly, Don Browning points to the inevitable contribution that culture makes to the moral context of a pastoral counselor.[27] Given the inextricability of theology from culture, the empirical approach to theology at least makes possible the above board examination of that relationship.

Finally, the empirical approach to theology acknowledges the dynamic character of theology. Theology is not simply an application of the past to the present, but involves history-making in Ross Snyder's sense.[28] An understanding of ministry is not, then, a restatement of the past, but a dynamic living in the present.

The vulnerabilities of an empirical approach to theology are the tendencies toward extreme relativism, faddism, and psychologizing. These vulnerabilities probably stem from the tendency of empirical theology to ignore or minimize the historical tradition. One cannot really say that empirical theologians ignore the historical tradition any more than one can say that the applied theologians ignore contemporary experience. The difference in emphasis is, however, a real difference.

The Christian education models growing out of empirical theology are inductive in that they attempt to draw meaning from the present situation. The planning process, for example, would begin with observing the situation and would proceed to analyzing, interpreting, and creating educational models that would respond to that situation. The models would likely include input on many subjects, including social issues and the human sciences. They would likely stress communication that would lead to what Snyder calls midwifing meaning,[29] or situational theologizing.[30] They would likely involve experiential exercises in which people would be encouraged to introspect and share their thoughts and feelings with others. They would likely encourage involvement and action in a wide variety of situations with people from many different perspectives. Finally, these models would likely involve acting, evaluating, and conceptualizing on the experiences.

Issues of Theological Method

Having reviewed two predominant approaches to theology, we can now see that the strict dichotomy between applied and empirical theology is clearly false. The applied, or normative, approach inevitably takes account of life experience, and the empirical inevitably takes account of historical understanding, at least in the sense of carrying some preconceived notions into its empirical observations. No theologian can conceivably limit his or her sources of authority to one source.[31] An empirical approach can never be untinged by the historical context nor can a normative approach be unaffected by the contemporary context.

The second methodological issue of concern here is how will theology relate to the past, present, and future in a meaningful synthesis? The applied mode tends to focus largely on the past for its theological formulations, and the empirical largely on the present. How can we bring these into dynamic interaction in our theologizing?

These issues are questions that call for new models of integration in the theological reflections of the Christian community. This is one of the most pressing needs if we are to rebuild the foundation of education in the traditioning community.

Conclusions for an Educational Model: The Traditioning Community

If the Christian church is to be both a preserving community and an agent of change, it must seek a theological method informed by both empirical and applied methodology and a model for integrating past, present, and future in its theological reflections. In recent years some very significant attempts have been made to theologize in light of the entire historical process, drawing together the witness of the historical tradition, of contemporary experience, and of future hope. These efforts have been enriched by new emphases that have emerged in theology, calling fresh attention to the historicity of the Christian community. The Latin American liberation theologians and the theologians of hope have both emphasized the crucial importance of future for the Christian faith community. Hope for God's future should guide and motivate our actions in the present. Several liberation and feminist theologians have called particular attention to the significance of present experience in the life of the community, both the way that experience influences our world view and the richness of meaning in that experience. Finally, we in Christian religious education are freshly reminded by those interested in religious socialization of the formative power of the community's past on its present. All these, taken together, force us to recognize the richness of our living tradition and urge us to work at creating models for theologizing that take all parts of that tradition seriously, including what is yet to be.

But how are people to get in touch with all those dimensions of tradition and to participate actively in it? What is being proposed here is an understanding of the church as an interpreting and transforming community. These are the two dominant functions of that community as it engages in traditioning. Both functions require the integration of past, present, and future. Interpretation is centered on proclaiming and reflecting, and transformation on acting in the church and in the world.

The Interpreting Community

The interpreting community seeks to understand. It does this by proclaiming and reflecting on the meaning of the community's witness of faith (past, present, and future) in light of the richest possible understanding of its own experience and that of the world. In its reflections, the community uses all available tools of analysis: historical, social, psychological, anthropological, political, and so forth.

Much attention has recently been given to interpretation through the study of the discipline of hermeneutics. Hermeneutics is usually translated "interpretation," and the words *interpretation* and *hermeneutics* will be used interchangeably here. *Hermeneutics* has rich connotations. It is often understood as "translation" or "explanation." The Greek verb *hermēneuein* can also be translated as "to proclaim" or "to speak." Hermeneutics, then, has to do with both proclamation and explanation. This double character relates it naturally to a traditioning community and to the education in that community. Education must necessarily be concerned with the community's expression and explanation of its faith.

As a discipline hermeneutics has been understood as the study of the principles of interpretation. It has traditionally included the three acts of discerning the meaning of the text in its original context (the meaning for its author and intended hearers), discerning the meaning of the text for the contemporary context, and moving according to certain principles or rules from the former to the latter.[32] James Sanders defines these three aspects of hermeneutics:

> (1) the principles, rules, and techniques whereby the interpreter of a text attempts to understand it in its original context; (2) the science of discerning how a thought or event in one cultural context may be understood in a different cultural context; and (3) the art of making the transfer.[33]

The discipline of hermeneutics, then, engages the text, the context, and the hermeneutical methods involved in moving from one to the other. This said, the unique problems in describing the hermeneutical dimensions of Christian religious education are problems of definition, of defining just what are the texts, the contexts, and the hermeneutical methods.

The Texts

The texts of hermeneutics have commonly been regarded as the biblical texts. In fact the definition of *hermeneutics* in *Webster's Third New International Dictionary* suggests this common understanding: "the study of the methodological principles of interpretation and explanation; *specif* : the study of the general principles of biblical interpretation." Many who speak of hermeneutics in relation to Christian religious education are primarily speaking of biblical interpretation.[34]

The question of texts has been opened up in recent years,[35] and we find many of the same questions of authority being raised as are raised in the tension between normative and empirical methods of theology. The texts of the traditioning model of education are taken to be inclusive of the biblical, historical, and contemporary witnesses of faith and the future hopes.

The Contexts

This question of the context of hermeneutics is one that has received relatively little attention until recent years. More attention has been given to the texts, including how to approach them and how to make the transfer from text to context. This introduces a problem because one cannot take for granted that the context is easily discerned and understood. The context is the situation in which and to which the text speaks. It is often ignored or studied only sketchily, but it is very important. The context influences the interpretation of the text at the same time that it is addressed by the text.

The tendency for persons to approach texts through a cultural preunderstanding, or conceptual framework, is being called freshly to attention by liberation and feminist theologians. Through these persons biblical hermeneutics is moving in new directions, taking more seriously the need to analyze the presuppositions one brings from the present context to the biblical-historical research. The contemporary context becomes important not only as the setting to which the historical texts speak but also as a guide for approaching and interpreting the texts (the methods, presuppositions, and so forth). The contexts are brought into dialogue with the texts, and the two are interpreted in light of each other.

In the traditioning model of religious education this kind of dialogue is held to be essential. The educational task is to facilitate that dialogue for persons who stand at a particular time and place interacting with many texts and contexts.

The Method

The question of hermeneutical method is of particular concern here because it has direct bearing on the continuity/change question. James Sanders recognizes that "[h]ermeneutics is the mid-point between the Bible's stability and adaptability as canon."[36] Whatever the hermeneutical method the question of stability and adaptability is raised, for the questions of the message arising from the text and its relationship to the present situation are inevitable. Sanders proposes to address this question through canonical hermeneutics.

> The task of biblical hermeneutics today is to seek a mid-point between the hermeneutical task of the historical-critical method, which seeks original biblical meanings, and the hermeneutical task of spanning the gap between those recovered meanings and modern cultural systems of meaning. And that task is called canonical hermeneutics: the means whereby Israel, Judaism, and the church spanned the gaps between inherited faith and new cultural settings.[37]

For Sanders the history of the canon itself offers a paradigm for the hermeneutical task. In the process by which the canon emerged, the earlier traditions and newer contexts were brought together, and the tradition itself was formed and re-formed. This is not unlike the proposal here that hermeneutics is a dialogic process out of which emerges fresh insight.

In both the demythologizing methods of Bultmann and the historical-critical methods of Emilio Betti and E. D. Hirsch, the adaptability of the text is understood to be more in its application to the contemporary situation. The original meaning is thought to be not only attainable in some sense but also unchangeable and universally applicable. For Sanders in his canonical hermeneutics, for Hans Gadamer in his dialectical approach to hermeneutics, and for Wolfhart Pannenberg in his theology of world history, the actual meaning of the historical texts is thought to change through history and through interaction with the different cultural contexts. Thus, the task of hermeneutics is to probe the way in which the tradition has been formed and re-formed. In these approaches the historical texts from every period are continually brought into dialogue with the contemporary witnesses of faith and the contemporary cultural context.

If a traditioning model of education has a hermeneutical dimension, then education needs to be dialogic, moving back and forth between the many witnesses of tradition and the personal and cultural dynamics of the present. This assumes that the earliest historical texts are not the only authoritative ones. This assumes that revelation continues through history and that the community's understanding at a given time is a synthesis of all the past, present, and future influences acting on the community.

The Transforming Community

The traditioning community seeks not only to understand, but also to act in the church and in the world. It seeks to act in the direction of the Kingdom of God, transforming and being transformed.[38] This idea is stressed particularly by the theologians of hope who point boldly to God's future and by the liberation theologians who point despairingly to the discrepancies between contemporary human existence and the ideal of the Kingdom of God. In the transforming community individuals, institutions, social organizations, and, indeed, all creation are transformed as people actively participate in the living tradition.

But what does this participation mean? We have said above that the traditioning community is related to God. The nature of this relationship is covenantal. It is a relationship of promise in which both God and God's people participate. It is a relationship that takes place in the midst of history.[39] And in this covenantal relationship are the seeds of transformation.

God's Promise

We have said above that the church is a community of promise living toward the future. This has been an historical emphasis in the understanding of the church and is finding revitalization under the present influences of Gustavo Gutiérrez, Jürgen Moltmann, and others. Both Gutiérrez and Moltmann emphasize that God is revealed through promise and that the future is the orienting focus of history.[40]

Moltmann calls attention to this futuristic orientation in the biblical message. God's appearance to Israel is never an end in itself but always points away from a particular time and place toward the future. In fact, Yahweh's appearance creates dissatisfaction with the present and movement toward future. "[T]he hearers of the promise become incongruous with the reality around them as they strike out in hope towards the promised new future. The result is not the religious sanctioning of the present, but a breaking away from the present towards the future."[41] The future is always before the people, and still in the New Testament message is a radical pointing forward. The gospel does not simply fulfill the Old Testament history of promises but itself points beyond to a new future: "In the gospel the Old Testament history of promise finds more than a fulfillment which does away with it; it finds its future."[42] Moltmann emphasizes the eschatological nature of Jesus' ministry and of the early Christian community. He thinks that the significance of this was not even understood by Schweizer, Weiss, and Barth who made so much of it. He suggests that the real significance of eschatology lies in the idea that hope springs from God's promise.[43] The Christian community, then, is a community of promise living toward God's future.

God's promise is real and related to the world but is not

without mystery. Gutiérrez points out that the liberation movement in Latin America holds forth a vision of the emancipation of persons and a "qualitatively different society."[44] At the same time he repeatedly points out the dialectical relationship between what he calls the Promise and the promises. God's promises are, indeed, fulfilled in history but cannot be completely identified with any particular social reality.[45]

God's promise in the fullest sense is the Kingdom of God, with all the wealth of meaning that term implies. God's promise carries with it an incentive for us to move in the direction of that Kingdom and an assurance of God's continuing presence with us.

The Church's Mission

If the church represents God's people (*ekklesia* and *laos*), then it must respond to and participate in God's promise. We must respond with hope and commitment. God's promise stands as the motivating force of our work, and also, as the judge of our efforts.[46] Our work will always seem partial and inadequate in light of the whole of God's promise.

The role of persons in bringing in the Kingdom is a fervidly debated issue. The position put forth here is that God's kingdom is a gift of God but human efforts do make a difference. God can work through persons, though human efforts will always be fallible and can never be equated with God's work. The position is similar to that of Thomas Groome.

> Thus while we can never claim to build the Kingdom by our own human efforts, yet those same efforts on behalf of human dignity, justice, freedom, and the like will bear fruit in the end. The Kingdom is a gift that comes by the grace of God. But the grace comes to us in our present to enable us to live lives that make the Kingdom present even now. By such lives we help prepare the "material" for its final realization. God is working out the Kingdom within our history, but not without the human activity that constitutes this history.[47]

What is the mission of the community then? Perhaps the mission of the church is doomed to be as elusive as the definition of the church. At least we can say at this point that the mission has to do with living in those images and models of the church discussed above. It has to do with being the people of God called out, the people who are engaged in sharing (koinonia), serving (*diakonia*), proclaiming (kerygma), and worshiping (*leitourgia*). Mission is not exactly the same in every age. It surely has to do with being deeply involved in people's suffering and engaged in actions that bear fruits of love, justice, and care for all creation. Definite, unchanging formulas for What should we do? elude us. We participate instead in the living stream of tradition that is the church. That involves some ambiguity and risk and demands full commitment.

If a traditioning model of education has a transformative dimension, then education needs to help people look forward and hope in God's promise. We need to proclaim those promises and to encourage people's inquiry and reflection on their meaning. We need, also, to enable persons to vision, plan, and act. Further, education needs to be deeply personal, encouraging teachers and students to relate in significant ways, to be open to God's spirit, and to be deeply involved in the persons and issues around them. In sum, we need to help people hear God's promises, participate actively in visioning, and be deeply involved with each other, God, and the world.

Summary of Assumptions About the Traditioning Community

The traditioning community is the context in which Christian religious education takes place. Our understanding of it is, therefore, foundational to our model of education. Below are four assumptions about that community that summarize the presentation in this chapter. These form foundations of the traditioning model proposed in part III.

1. The images and models of the church are rich, reflecting its many dimensions and the mystery that is inherent in it.
2. The nature of the church is historical. It is deeply influenced by its past, present, and future and cannot escape its temporality. As a historical community, it relates to God, relates to the world, bears tradition, and lives toward the future.
3. The community has a theologizing task that requires the study of the historical tradition, contemporary experience, and future hope. The duality between applied and empirical methods of theology needs to be transcended so that the community can be encouraged to search for the meanings in the past, present, and future.
4. The community's educational task is to involve persons in the living Christian tradition. This involves the interpretive tasks of proclaiming and reflecting on the meanings in the Christian witness. It also includes the transformative tasks of acting in the direction of God's kingdom.

In part III these assumptions about the church will be implicit as formative factors in the educational model proposed there.

The Person in Process

The good old days were those in which persons seemed to change in a gradual process and the challenge for educators was to encourage people in their changing. The problem in recent days seems different, for the human community seems to change in dramatic and unlimited ways.

The landscape of human values, institutions, beliefs, and practices will hardly stand still long enough for scientists to describe them. Certainly some of these values, institutions, beliefs, and practices seem peculiarly resistant to change, and we marvel at their tenacity. At the same time we hear of people's struggling to adapt to the rapidly changing world, often struggling to find some unchanging core they can grasp as the world around them flashes with new issues of global justice and resource depletion, new kinds of life-style options, new products to buy, and new products not to buy because they may be harmful to their health. Dwayne Huebner states that "the problem is no longer one of explaining change, but of explaining nonchange. Man is a transcendent being, i.e., he has the capacity to transcend what he is to become something that he is not."[1]

And so one foundational issue for the formulation of a model of Christian religious education is the question of the nature of persons. Are persons primarily static or changing? Are they individualistic or communal? Are they active or passive? These questions cannot really be separated from similar questions concerning the nature of reality, i.e., the nature of the world in which persons exist. The world is not simply a backdrop for the human drama but is itself part of the drama of creation. Persons are part of this whole of creation, so we must ask: Is the world primarily static or changing? Is it a collection of unrelated parts or a web of interrelated entities? Is it active or passive?

The search for a model of education that maximizes the possibility for continuity and change calls for us to grapple with these issues. The traditioning model emerging here is based on certain assumptions about the nature of persons that will be probed in this chapter.

Questions About Human Nature

In probing the possible views of human persons, one can see quickly that the options can be dichotomized (and have been) as easily as can be the phenomena of continuity and change. Three kinds of questions about human nature will be of particular concern here.

Are Persons Stable or Changing?

The answer to this first question may be less simple and obvious than it seems. For many years psychologists and sociologists have focused on the static aspects of human nature, i.e., the essential nature of human persons. The search has been for definitions of qualities such as personality, intelligence, patterns of group formation and maintenance, interaction styles, and patterns of learning. Even developmental psychologists, who have studied human change, have largely focused on the static states, or stages, of the developmental continuum. In an attempt to generalize, psychologists and sociologists have tested their hypotheses in different cultures but always with the idea of finding universals, the essential aspects of human nature that transcend cultural boundaries. The static and universal aspects have been the focus, with the changing aspects taking a secondary role.

In recent years some shift has been taking place away from

this perspective, particularly as more attention is given to the dynamics of change. In developmental psychology, for example, Erik Erikson took a large step in this direction by emphasizing the psychosocial aspects of human development. Far more than Freud, Erikson has focused on the actual process of development and on the dynamic interaction of the internal psychological and external social factors in this process. Similarly, Jean Piaget has attended to the processes of assimilation and accommodation by which development proceeds.

Even more radical shifts are taking place, though, as psychological and sociological theories are taken to task for their biases toward the fixity of the world. Proponents of phenomenological sociology, for example, criticize contemporary sociology for its "view of the methodology as a set of techniques to be used to catch the unchanging properties of a 'solid' factual world."[2] In their desire to interpret the meaning of everyday experience the phenomenologists want to avoid imposing preset assumptions about a fixed world and fixed categories on our questions and our methods.

Similarly, Klaus Riegel has proposed a dialectical theory of development that "seeks to understand the changing individual in a changing social world."[3] He is not concerned with the stable characteristics of persons or with the fixed patterns of development. He is concerned, rather, with the dynamics of human change. He has proposed that development takes place through the interacting influences of events that are inner-biological, individual-psychological, cultural-sociological, and outer-physical.[4] The developmental changes are never-ending, taking place as change in one dimension produces disharmony in another. A contradiction is set up (e.g., between the biological maturation and the cultural expectations), and a crisis results. The resolution yields a new synthesis, e.g., a new perspective or a new pattern of relating. Riegel recognizes that this approach to developmental psychology shifts the focus from the developmental levels of stability to the dynamics of change.

Unlike Piaget's theory of cognitive development, a dialectical theory of development does not emphasize the plateaus at which equilibrium or balance is achieved. Stable plateaus of balance are the exception, a temporary marking or achievement. As soon as a developmental task is completed and synchrony attained, new questions, doubts, and contradictions arise within the individual and within society.[5]

The question, then, in our era is wide open. Are persons stable in certain essential characteristics, or are they characterized more fundamentally by continuing change?

Are Persons Individual or Social?

A second kind of question about human nature has to do with relatedness. To what extent are persons related to others and the world, and what is the nature of the relationhip? Is it superficial or internal? The answers to these questions have often been dichotomized in recent years. The individualistic and communal points of view have been placed in opposition.

Donald Campbell has raised questions about one form of this dichotomizing in his presidential address to the American Psychological Association.[6] He suggests that the psychologists' emphasis on persons as individual, self-gratifying, biological organisms has led to a distrust of the social restraint imposed by moral traditions. The psychological view has tended to devalue the role of social institutions and of traditions on persons' lives and to place great value on the importance of self-gratification, pleasure, and so forth. This view emerged in opposition to another viewpoint in which persons were thought to be in need of the restraint that society's traditions offer. The psychological point of view has placed great trust in the basic goodness of the human organism, and the latter has assumed a basic inadequacy or weakness in human nature that calls for social restraint. Campbell suggests that the psychological view he describes may be demonstrated scientifically to be inadequate. Studies of population genetics and of social system evolution give renewed credibility to the social and personal value of the so-called "repressive or inhibitory moral traditions."[7]

This conflict between a modern psychological and a traditional moral perspective need not be discussed in the abstract. People hold these opposing views in an endless variety of forms. In the extreme of the modern psychological point of view, persons resist all forms of social boundedness and seek self-gratification as an end in itself. Therefore, relationships, commitments, ideologies, social mores, and traditional rituals and restraints are understood to be secondary to this push toward self-gratification or some other individualistic goal.

Robert Lifton describes just such a reality when he describes "protean man."[8] The protean person seeks to be relieved of social restraints in order to explore the new.

> What has actually disappeared—in Sartre and in protean man in general—is the classic superego, the internalization of clearly defined criteria of right and wrong transmitted within a particular culture by parents to their children. Protean man requires a freedom from precisely that kind of superego—he requires a symbolic fatherlessness—in order to carry out his explorations.[9]

The protean person is a new kind of person who is in a continual process of re-creation and who, in short, is continually seeking change over continuity. Lifton suggests that historic shifts have disrupted persons' relationship to their social institutions and symbols, thereby causing "historical (or psychohistorical) dislocation."[10] At the same time persons have been exposed to a "flooding of imagery" so that they are bombarded by partial and superficial alternatives to the cultural institutions and symbols.[11] They are, in short, under the illusion that one can separate himself or herself from the restraints and obligations of culture and that this is a desirable state.

If the individualistic point of view is one extreme, then the communal point of view is the other. In the extreme of the latter, social institutions and values are thought to be the shapers of individual persons and the real source of human value. The behaviorists have particularly worked under the assumption that persons are formed by the environment of people, things, and events outside themselves with little if any influence coming from within. The consequent emphasis is not on individuality, but on the influence of society and the outer environment on the individual.

Are Persons Active or Passive?

The third question about human nature is whether persons actively engage the world or are passively formed by it. Again, this issue has been called to attention by the modern social sciences. The corresponding question is whether the environment in which persons live is active or passive. One's answers to these questions have a great deal to do with one's educational model, for it affects one's assumptions about the learners and the educational environment.

Klaus Riegel has analyzed four perspectives of human development.[12] In the first, both the persons and the environment are seen as passive, and development takes place only through association of stimuli. In the second, the persons are thought to be active and the environment passive, and development takes place as persons actively explore their environment. Piaget represents this point of view. In the third, the persons are thought to be passive and the environment active, as in Skinner's behavior modification. Finally, in the fourth point of view, both the persons and the environment are thought to be actively influencing each other. Riegel praises the Soviet psychologist S. L. Rubinstein for putting forth this alternative. In this point of view the interactive relationship between the individual and society is emphasized.

So the question of human freedom emerges in terms of how active are people in engaging the world or how passive they are in being molded by it. We must also address the old puppet-on-a-string question in relation to God. Are persons active or passive in relation to God?

Toward a Process Model of Human Nature

Here we will probe into a process model of persons with the hope of suggesting new ways of thinking about human existence and about education. The hope is that we can transcend these dichotomous ways of thinking about human nature.

Imagine the person in process, moving into an intersection. This person is part of the traffic flow moving in one direction. But in the intersection, the person is faced with traffic and pedestrians from all directions, with traffic signals, with a memory of traffic rules, with personal concerns that may be faraway, with road conditions, and with who knows what else. The person can continue moving in the same direction or turn or stop or speed ahead. That person will be influenced, of course, by his or her own plans and may simply follow these. But the person will also be influenced by what is happening in the intersection. The plans may be changed or even forgotten. This is the person in process, living through a succession of intersections.

The three basic assumptions proposed here correspond to the three questions raised above.

1. Are persons stable or changing? The answer is both. They are somehow continuous with their past and somehow changing as they move into their future. The person at the intersection is faced with the decision to continue according to plan or to change course. Both options are real, and either decision will be influenced by what has gone before, what is happening in the intersection, and what is anticipated about the future. Whether the person continues or changes course, the forces for continuity and the forces for change will have played their part in the drama.

2. Are persons individual or social? I am proposing that persons are internally related to God, to other persons, and to the world. God and the world enter deeply into our own individual goals and plans and into the changes that are made in these along the way.
3. Finally, are persons active or passive? I am proposing that persons are both acting and acted upon by God and the world around them. We are not passive spectators at the intersection. We are acting and being acted upon all the way through.

This is the proposed model of human nature. These three assumptions will be examined and elaborated through the rest of this chapter.

These three assumptions actually spring from various soils. The first assumption about the processive nature of reality is characteristic not only of the process philosophy of Whitehead and Hartshorne but also of pragmatism. Eugene Fontinell recognizes the value of all these new philosophies in pushing toward a deeper understanding of process and in recognizing that "reality is processive through and through."[13] In an attempt to reconcile the continuity and change of reality, philosophers have largely viewed change as a superficial or secondary phenomenon. Fontinell notes:

In both philosophy and religion the unchanging, the permanent, the eternal, the timeless have been the treasured goals. Change and time were to be overcome, or, at best, seen as pathways to a reality beyond. Whether referring to the cosmos, to man or to God, the grand assumption was that each was essentially complete. Whatever change was conceded to the first two (God, of course, was allowed no change at all) was relegated to the surface, was "accidental," as compared to the unchanging principles, laws and values which "essentially" constituted them.[14]

If, however, reality is viewed as processive through and through, then the challenge is to explain continuity and stability. The challenge is to understand the relationship between continuity and change.

The second assumption about the relatedness of God, persons, and the world is picked up by the pragmatists as well as by the psychologists discussed above, S. L. Rubinstein and Klaus Riegel. Though Rubinstein and Riegel do not deal with the relatedness with God, they go far in emphasizing the relatedness of all reality by suggesting that persons develop through complex interactions between the internal biochemical and the external sociocultural processes.[15] These are not parallel processes, but interacting ones. Riegel adds an emphasis on the physical world to this complex of interactions. Persons develop in relation to both internal and external forces.

The last assumption is that God, persons, and the world are all active in their relationships with each other. Both Rubinstein and Riegel see human persons and the environment in a dynamic interaction in which both are active participants. Neither of these men, however, takes account of the role of God in this complex of relationships.

And so we have clues as to how we might break out of some customary patterns of thinking about human nature, but many questions are left unanswered. We will leave these questions for now and explore the work of two persons who have particularly focused on the processive quality of reality. George Herbert Mead in his social psychology and Alfred North Whitehead in his metaphysics have both offered clues for the understanding of human persons and for a model of education that might stimulate both continuity and change.

George Herbert Mead:
A Social-Psychological View

We look first to George Herbert Mead. Mead was unique in defining the self in terms of a process rather than as a static entity. The concept of self was derived originally from the Anglo-Saxon word meaning "same" or "identical." The idea of self then suggests a particular identity that exists through time. Mead's uniqueness was his basic idea that social interactions produce a developing, rather than a static, self.[16] In this concept of self are clues as to how continuity and change can coexist without the one's destroying the other.

Mead understood his own work against the background of the scientists and philosophers in the ancient world who sought reality in the essence of an object.[17] Mead was attempting to describe the world as it was implied by the scientific method and seeking to know the changing form of the world.[18]

Mead's Basic Understanding of Reality

Mead describes the world as continually passing, and the unit of existence is called an event or an act.[19] Change, however, implies identity as well, for without identity change would not even be recognized as different.[20]

Mead understands reality not only as continually changing but as being affected by human intelligence. Mead suggests that the scientific method is "the evolutionary process grown self-conscious."[21] The scientific method offers a method of progress by offering a means for analyzing problems and testing solutions. Mead sees this as a means for enabling change and, also, for maintaining structure and order.

Mead's theory is based on the idea that the present is the locus of reality.[22] The present is an emergent event in which the past is written and the foundations for the future are laid. The emergent event is "more than the processes that have led up to it," but it is an event that is itself unique.[23] As such it contributes to the possibilities of the future.

The Development of the Self

Given this basic understanding of reality, Mead would naturally view the nature of the self as processive. The self derives from the social process and, in turn, affects that process. Certain features of human development particularly shed light on the relationship between continuity and change.

Development Is the Internalization of Social Control

First, the development of the self is a process of taking the roles of others into oneself, of internalizing social control. Individuals develop as they begin to internalize society's expectations and attitudes toward them. "For social psychology, the whole (society) is prior to the part (the individual), not the part to the whole; and the part is explained in terms of the whole, not the whole in terms of the part or parts."[24] This viewpoint has come to characterize the symbolic interaction theory of socialization that has grown up from Mead's work.[25] Mead thinks that his understanding is akin to the behaviorist view, with the additional focus on the inner side of behavior.[26] A social act, then, is a complex process that involves stimulus, response, and the internal processes of thinking.

The internalization of social control takes place as a person learns to "take the role of the other." This is a conversation that takes place within individuals as they take the roles and attitudes of others into their own thoughts. The person at the intersection recalls the warnings, attitudes, and advice that have been experienced in the past, and these enter into the inner conversation. This inner conversation is what Mead means by thought.[27]

The process of taking the role of the other leads to a person's development of a social self (or an image of oneself from another's perspective). A person perceives, for example, that others think of him or her as a good person, an underachiever, the bad one in the family, and so forth. Each of these images is called a me. One will, of course, have more than one such me. These may include the attitudes and expectations from mother, father, the local congregation, the fifth-grade teacher, the high school group of friends, and so forth.

But we are not passively molded by these attitudes of other people. These various images of one's social self are coordinated by the I (or subjective self) that responds to the various me's.[28] As we stand at the intersection we may be bombarded with images of ourselves as others see us (good girl, nice boy, naughty child, special friend, lazy worker), and we have to respond to these. All the persons and groups of persons who touch our lives influence us, and we as individuals have to sift and sort through all these influences and make choices for our life.

The process of taking the role of the other is a complex interaction between the social images of oneself (me's) and one's subjective self (I). This is the way people develop and the way they can take account of the various factors of past, present, and future.[29] This also makes possible the complex interactions in human society. Persons develop the ability to take to themselves the attitude not only of a particular other but also of the generalized other (such as the church or the school). As persons take the role of these others they internalize their view about God, church, sex, democracy, and so forth. These influences become part of the person's experience from which they can draw. The persons (with their subjective I self) are always engaged in selecting and interpreting.

Development Is Influenced by Symbols

The second feature to note in Mead's understanding of the self is that development is influenced by symbols created in social interaction. As pointed out above, thinking is a conversation with oneself, taking the attitude of the other and utilizing significant symbols.[30] Persons communicate significant symbols to one another through gestures, including speech, music, rituals, body movements, and so forth. Persons thus call out an attitude in others and in themselves when they exchange these symbols (such as a smile or a handshake).[31]

A significant symbol is one that has a common meaning for everyone involved. The person at the intersection, for example, recognizes the red light and knows what it signifies. Similarly, the following incident reflects the functioning of significant symbols.

Walking along a seashore in Wales, I was struck by the power of significant symbols. I heard a group of people singing hymns and noticed that several people stopped to join in. Others walked on past but joined in the singing as well, carrying the tune on down the promenade. I lingered and listened, but when the singing ended and the sermon began people began to wander off. The sermon was an ordinary sidewalk type with the usual theme and the usual words and style. Its power as a significant symbol with this group (or as a positive symbol anyway) was far less great than that of the hymn, which was familiar to so many of these folk and which apparently entered into their own inner conversations with significant communities in their own history.

Through the dynamic exchange of significant symbols and through the incorporation of these into thought, persons form opinions of their own. "The formation of opinion takes place through conversation of individuals with members of groups to which they belong or through that inner conversation of thought which is outer conversation imported into the mind."[32] This same basic process works in human institutions. The institutions of church, school, or family can be regarded as social habits or patterns that are communicated through significant symbols (such as the liturgy of the church, the daily routines of the school, or the private jokes of the family). These symbols arouse certain responses in the individual participants.[33] The institutions, then, help form the thoughts and opinions of the individual persons.

In practical terms for Christian education, this would suggest that the symbols communicated through the gestures of the communion ritual call forth certain responses in the community of worshipers. The exchange of gestures in the ritual shapes the common life of the community. Likewise, the gestures in speech and writing on such subjects as marriage or political involvement call forth responses in the participants of the institution. The responses may be different for different participants, however, e.g., apathy, action, or rebellion. Self-consciousness comes about when one reflects on and analyzes why symbols call up different responses in others than in oneself.[34]

The most significant point here is that the influence of the group is related to its language and symbols. A group has more influence on the individual when the two speak the same language, i.e., when the symbols are significant (or mutually understood) for both the group and the individual.[35] Mead recognizes that leaders and writers must communicate in the language of the persons they address if they wish to evoke response. The task of the religious educator would be to communicate in significant symbols of the group and to seek ways to make the traditional symbols of the church significant for the contemporary group.

Development Is Influenced by Complex Interactions

The third feature in Mead's understanding of the development of the self is that social relationships are interactive. What one person does affects another and vice versa. This is similar to Rubinstein and Riegel's idea that human persons and the environment are in a dynamic interaction and that both are active participants in the interaction. The person is not passively created by social forces, but is a product of the social process in which he or she is an active part.

The complexity of interaction can be seen in the process of exchanging gestures. When one person says a cheery hello to another, the second person responds. The latter is influenced by the kind of greeting that has been given but also by his or her own physical and mental state. This means that the second person's response may be a grunt rather than a cheery hello. This grunt, then, triggers reactions in the first person, who chooses another response. Each person is being influenced by the other but also by his or her internal thought processes. The interaction is a "mutual adjustment of changing social response to changing social stimulation."[36] One gesture calls forth a response gesture, which, in turn, calls forth another gesture, and so on. The gestures modify one another as they emerge. In this way persons influence each other.

Persons may be conscious of their own attitudes in this process of interaction. They may analyze their own response to various stimuli and adjust the response accordingly. At the same time, persons can be conscious that their own attitudes affect the response of the other person, so that they can potentially exert a certain amount of control over the other's response. Mead suggests that one's influence on others is affected, in fact, by one's own self-awareness and intentionality in the interaction process.[37] This means not that one person can manipulate another as a puppet, but that people can influence others to a greater or lesser degree and can be more influential if they are self-conscious about it.

Development Is Influenced by Meaning

A fourth feature in Mead's understanding of the developing self is that meaning is created in the interaction. Persons become conscious of their own attitudes in the interaction, and this is their sense of meaning.[38] Persons are actively interpreting what is going on, and these interpretations affect what they do. This suggests that meaning emerges only in a social act in which a person is aware of his or her own contribution and attitude. Disengagement does not lead to a sense of meaning.

Meanings are formed and re-formed as persons interact with others. Persons attempt to make sense of the world as they have experienced it and to reformulate their thoughts when new meanings emerge in experience that do not fit with the old. In short, persons apply the scientific method in their thinking,[39] and meanings are constantly being revised.

Meanings are also communicated through the symbols of one's social group or culture.[40] Culture, in fact, exists as a vast set of shared meanings and values that influence how we act. Likewise, our actions may lead to some alteration in the culture's meanings and values.

The Self as Dynamic

All this is to say that persons inherit from the past and the social group but are also involved in selecting stimuli and creating their own environment. In their responses they may take account of the future as well. The nature of human intelligence is "that it builds up its future out of its past."[41] Human persons influence the past by selecting those stimuli from the past to which to respond, and they influence the future by self-consciously responding in the present so as to influence the future responses of others and themselves.

This relationship that the self has with past, present, and future is not a magical one. It is one that develops as the self stands in the present, which is overlapped by past and future. Mead calls this overlapping sociality, which suggests a social relationship between the past and the future as they come together in the present. The coming together is basic to the nature of reality. "The social character of the universe we find in the situation in which the novel event is in both the old order and the new which its advent heralds. Sociality is the capacity of being several things at once."[42]

Again it must be emphasized that for Mead meaning exists in the present. His understanding of sociality is that the present is where the past and the future come together. "This view then frees us from bondage either to past or future. We are neither creatures of the necessity of an irrevocable past, nor of any vision given in the Mount. . . . Our values lie in the present, and past and future give us only the schedule of the means, and the plans of campaign for their realization."[43] This view frees us to root deeply into our past, to dream dreams for the future, and to live in both of these worlds in the present.

Educationally, this view suggests the importance of presenting a rich heritage, of reenacting traditional rituals, of encouraging speculation and dreaming about the future, of thinking through ideological visions, and of considering how all these inform our present actions.

In general, Mead's social psychology is rich in educational implications that have never been thoroughly mined. Douglas Kimmel does draw implications that three types of experience may be particularly important to symbolic interaction in persons: (a) situation experience, offering a greater number of situations from which persons can learn and draw; (b) interaction experience, leading to a greater ability to take the role of the other and to interpret significant symbols; and (c) self-experience, leading to a greater ability to see oneself from another's point of view and to build one's self-knowledge.[44] These types of experience are highly suggestive of what a model of Christian religious education needs to include.

Alfred North Whitehead: A Metaphysical View

Alfred North Whitehead offers into this dialogue a metaphysical system. He understands reality itself to be a dynamic interaction between continuity and change. Most significant is Whitehead's fundamental notion that all reality is in process and that this process is a succession of discrete events. Continuity is real but emerges in this succession of events rather than being characteristic of substances.

This does not mean that we perceive the world as isolated events, for events are linked together.[45] Each event inherits from preceding ones and passes on that inheritance to future ones (continuity). Novelty is also introduced, and as the different elements of the past and future are brought together in the new event a new synthesis takes place (change). This is the nature of the creative process.[46] All the elements of past and future enter into the new event. "The many become one and are increased by one."[47]

Whitehead understands reality to be a process with continuity and change. He urges that any interpretation of reality must take account of both permanence and flux, order and originality.[48] Both of these polarities are noteworthy to the Christian educator who must choose how much to emphasize learning the historical tradition and clearly ordered ideas and how much to emphasize immediate experience and imaginative thinking.

Whitehead affirms that "the art of progress is to preserve order amid change, and to preserve change amid order."[49] In saying this, he is clearly not suggesting a choice between permanence and flux, nor a "taking turns" between the two. In fact, he criticizes philosophy for giving its attention only to flux or only to permanence or for "a wavering balance between the two."[50]

What Whitehead is saying is that order and disorder are necessary correlates, both being essential for intensity of experience.[51] This suggests that religious education that focuses only on the "fundamental lasting truths" or only on the immediate experiences of the group is destined to become lifeless and useless. The lasting truths will suffer from loss of relevance, and the immediate experiences will suffer from lack of rootedness.

Clues about how these contrasting qualities are held together can be found in Whitehead's understanding of process. We now turn our attention to this.

Basic Processes Enabling Continuity and Change

Whitehead speaks of two kinds of processes. The macroscopic processes take place from one event to another. The microscopic processes take place within a given event. Both processes have elements of continuity and of change.

Macroscopic Process

Macroscopic processes typically take place when an event (or occasion) emerges from its past. An aerial view of the intersection would reveal movement from one moment to the next. This is the change created by the macroscopic process. Change takes place when the emerging occasion is somehow different from occasions that went before. Persons, for example, may change direction. According to Whitehead, the persons have not changed, but their courses have changed as a result of the influences on them and/or their decisions. In the succession of events, change is simply the emergence of new events or entities.[52]

Whitehead wants to discard the idea of enduring substances without discarding the ideas that there are both endurance and change in experience. "We have certainly to make room in philosophy for the contrasted notions, one that every actual entity endures, and the other that every morning is a new fact with its measure of change."[53] Each emerging event involves some continuity (repetition of the earlier events) and some change (transformation of these past data into something novel).

Microscopic Process

The microscopic process is the integration process that takes place within a given event as it receives objective data and transforms these into a new unity. This is revealed, not through an aerial view of the intersection, but through a close-up view of the emerging event. It is described as the process by which the many become one.[54] This simply means that all the influences of the past are synthesized into the new event.

Each emerging event is influenced by its past but also has a "subjective aim," which is its own individual purpose and which gives direction to its becoming.[55] The data of the past make possible continuity, and the subjective aim makes possible the subject's own unique decision.

This microscopic process is analogous to the interaction of the objective me and the subjective I in Mead's description of the process of human development. The entity has the potential for continuity in its inheritance of the given past and the potential for change in the individual decision it makes as it brings together the past in a new and unique unity. As a new event it becomes data for other emerging events, thus adding its own uniqueness to the potential of the future.[56]

Complex Phenomena Contributing to Continuity and Change

In addition to the basic macroscopic and microscopic processes, Whitehead describes some more complex phenomena that have bearing on continuity and change. A brief look at the phenomena of novelty, endurance, and contrast will illumine the above discussion and introduce some of the complexities and possibilities.

Novelty

The phenomenon of novelty has been mentioned above. Whitehead suggests that each event is novel in itself.[57] This means that every entity is in some way, however small, different from all that has gone before or will follow. As we saw above, an entity is never simply the sum of its physical parts (i.e., its inheritance of the past, objective world). An entity also has a mental pole that influences the way in which the various elements are integrated.[58]

The presence of novelty gives insight into how God is involved in becoming occasions, i.e., as "the ground of all order and of all originality."[59] God contributes novelty to the emerging event. God is present in the world and is part of the reality to be experienced. Further, God influences the subjective aim of each emerging event. Each event stands in relationship to God, and what the event inherits from the past is transformed as God calls forward to new possibilities.[60]

Novelty can break into reality in unexpected ways, but it

can then be passed from event to event, from generation to generation. The Exodus was a novel event in the life of Israel, but the novelty became part of the tradition as it was preserved in the shared memory of the people.

The cumulation of memory can also explain personal identity through time.[61] Persons' identities are tied to their memories, and the richness of their memories contributes to the richness of their personhood. This is similar to Mead's view that the cumulation of me's affects the development of the self.

Endurance

Contrasted with novelty is the phenomenon of endurance, the process of passing on particular characteristics from one actual occasion to another. This process is part of human existence,[62] so persons have many aspects of themselves that do not seem to change much through time, such as their physical appearance, their ways of responding to stress, their central religious beliefs, and so forth.

Whitehead has given us clues to explain both radical change through novelty and persistent characteristics through endurance. We are left now with the task of understanding the relationship between this novelty and this endurance. Whitehead observes that there is no evidence that unwavering endurance (or pure continuity with the past) is even possible.[63] An inevitable tension exists between novelty and enduring structure.

A person embodies both the repetitive and originative processes,[64] which are integrated and coordinated in persons through central occasions, the succession of which constitutes the living person, or the "enduring personality."[65]

Contrast

If human persons are defined in terms of both continuity and change, the question arises as to how these two are balanced or synthesized. What happens in a given event when the forces of the past and the forces of novelty meet? Whitehead's idea of "contrast" is particularly fruitful in approaching this question.

A contrast is the means by which radically different influences are brought together into unity.[66] An example of a contrast would be the dilemma faced by a boy entering a new school. He knows how he made friends in his former school but cannot do so in his new school. The contrast for this student would be the working out of new behavior that takes account of both his old patterns and the demands of the new situation. In this case, the old patterns could ruin his chances for making friends in the new school, but complete conformity to the expectations of the new school could mean the loss of his own sense of integrity. What is called for is a new synthesis that involves both continuity with his past and change for his present situation. This could be a radical change in his behavior in this new situation, a decision to seek friends outside the school, or any number of changes in between.

A contrast makes possible an event being informed by a maximal amount of data, with as little data as possible being ignored or dismissed. The result is a decision that has some kind of order, unity, and harmony.[67] This is an important phenomenon in human development. Persons normally develop in the direction of increased complexity, i.e., toward high forms of order in which the growing wealth of experience and novelty are held together. This takes place in the process of converting opposition into contrast.

Process as a Social Phenomenon

All that has been said about process leads back to the emphasis that all process is social. By social we mean that all events are interrelated.[68] The events of the past become incorporated in the new event as it forms.

Whitehead's view of process as social has some radical implications for our understanding of the present. For Whitehead, a person's relationship to the past and future is never an exercise in abstraction. The past and future actually enter into the present. This explains why old memories come back to haunt us and dreams pull us forward. Whitehead's idea is closely akin to Mead's concept of sociality. The emerging occasion lives in both worlds, experiencing the past and anticipating the future.[69] The integration of continuity and change, then, takes place in the emerging events. In order to facilitate integration we must create conditions that are conducive to the emerging occasion's own synthesizing process.

Reality as Dynamic

The implications of this exploration of Whitehead's metaphysics are vast, but a few will be highlighted that are particularly relevant to a model of education.

One implication of the interrelatedness of past, present, and future is that Christian religious educators can never ignore any of these. In our time, much of the futurist movement does attempt to deny the past. Such an effort is neither desirable nor possible. Likewise, one cannot ignore the future. Norman Pittenger considers the Christian church itself as a social process and suggests that we in the church live in the present, from the past, and toward the future.[70] An educational model drawing from this insight would recognize the interconnectedness of past, present, and future and would seek to enhance persons' awareness and integration of all three.

Charles Hartshorne adds to this idea when he says, "How we look backward is how we decide forward."[71] This suggests that movement forward requires an awareness of where we have been. This means that turning over a new leaf requires thorough reading in the earlier pages of one's book. It implies that revitalizing Christian religious education requires serious study of earlier modes of religious education. It implies that educating people for the 1980s and 90s requires helping them understand and evaluate the 1950s, 60s, and 70s as well as earlier centuries.

Finally, Whitehead's understanding of the role of dogma reveals something of the dynamic interplay he sees between permanence and flux, continuity and change. "A system of dogmas may be the ark within which the Church floats safely down the flood-tide of history. But the Church will perish unless it opens its window and lets out the dove to search for an olive branch."[72] We can expand Whitehead's metaphor and recognize ourselves floating in this ark filled with animals that we so graciously brought on board and cannot now get rid of. We can be grateful that on our journey, which is so laden with the decisions of our past, we can indeed open a window and launch a new search. We can be even more grateful that God has placed a rainbow over our search, filled with promises that draw us forward.

Conclusions for an Educational Model

Having explored some of the generalities and technicalities of Mead's and Whitehead's thought, we can now attempt to draw together the insights into human nature. Drawing from Mead's social psychology and Whitehead's metaphysics, we come to a dynamic view of persons' development that has fruitful implications for Christian religious education.

The aim of these concluding remarks is to draw together some central insights and to propose a model of human nature that will inform education. Hopefully, these insights will inform our work in such everyday contexts as this one:

I teach a group of sixth-graders in our church. I walked in the first week with a well-made plan, but the meeting was a dreadful disappointment for me and for the children too, I am sure. In frustration I later reflected on the morning. All the typical answers rushed through my thoughts. I immediately assumed that something had to be fixed so that the next meeting would go better.

Then, I heard my inner voice of protest, *I don't want your easy answers. Don't tell me about the latest teaching method or tightening up on discipline,* and a loud *No* to the equally easy answer of giving up on the church school altogether.

I thought about these children who come to this place with so many different expectations, expectations that Sunday school is always dull, that church is a place to go because their parents make them, that the only way to tolerate this system is to undermine it, and fears that no one will listen to them here. These children have varied histories, some of which carry quite a lot of pain. These children live in a culture where church-going is unusual, certainly not a widely accepted part of life. They are part of a church that focuses its ministry largely on adults. These children have been stimulated more than regulated, having traveled, read, lived in the media culture, and participated in countless activities. These are children who know little of the Jewish and Christian story. Oh, they know something about a few key biblical characters and something about the life of their own church, but they know nothing of the two thousand years of Christian tradition between the New Testament church and the present. And they know little or nothing about the life of the church universal in the world today. They do know that the issues of the world are large and that the future is threatened by hunger, poverty, political turmoil, and war.

In short, these children are living in relationship to many persons, to their own histories, to a historical faith tradition, to a local faith community, to a complex world of political struggle, war, and injustices, and to a very uncertain future.

This is where religious education must begin, right in the middle, at the intersection. Religious education must begin where person meets person, where person faces future, where person probes past, where person confronts contemporary issues. Persons stand in relationship to God and in relation to the world of past, present, and future. To begin education anywhere other than the middle of these relationships is to split off some segment of life and artificially treat it in isolation from every other part.

The old life-experience-to-Bible or Bible-to-life-experience debate is antiquated. Neither the Bible nor present life experience should be the starting point for Christian religious education. The starting point is the intersection, and at this intersection are not only the Bible and the present life experience of individuals but parents, church folk, the historical church tradition, the fears and hopes for the future of the world, the culture in which the church exists, the issues of the global village, and God. That intersection is a big place. It is an awesome place, and none of us can think of it without some fear. This is where we minister.

Assumptions About Human Nature

But how do we describe that intersection so that it helps us know what to do in education? Here we return to the three basic assumptions put forth earlier. They can now be elaborated under the influence of Mead, Whitehead, and countless others.

Assumption 1. The persons at the intersection are in process. They are somehow continuous with their past and somehow changing as they move into their future.

Educationally, this suggests that an individual is never finished and that persons have opportunities for transformation at all points in their lives. This suggests further that persons are influenced by both past events and future possibilities. Teachers, then, need to highlight both, rather than to look purely backward or forward, if they are to stimulate and guide students' self-development.[73]

Proposition 1. God is active in that process. Persons develop in the midst of a continuing succession of events in which God is always active.

God is experienced in each event as part of the objective past and future possibility and as the guiding force to the process. God has been, will be, and is now. God does not determine the process but guides it through persuasive love.

This suggests that neither education nor any other ministry of the church is a fully human enterprise. God is in, under, and above them all. The human work may be moved and guided by God but should not be confused with God's work. God's work transcends human efforts, and human efforts are never identical with God's work. This idea of God's transcending power keeps the educational ministry in perspective so that we do not take ourselves too seriously. It also offers a hope that pulls always to the future, a hope that God will lead us, will transform our meager efforts into something of worth, and will act unceasingly in the world to create and redeem.

Proposition 2. Each event in the process involves decision. The past, present, and future come together in the new occasion, and the way these come together is a decision of the occasion itself and is unique to it.

The rich young ruler wants to inherit eternal life. He meets Jesus at the intersection. He has long lived with the commands of God and is confronted now by the challenge of Jesus. The decision is the man's. It has to be made now at the intersection.

Educationally, this reminds us that the teacher cannot force decision. The teacher cannot even force a certain interpretation of the past or future on anyone else. The task is to enhance the potential within the persons or group to make their own decisions, rather than to prepackage a decision and try to "sell" it. This means that a teacher must learn to let go of an idea or an experience and allow the students or group to deal with it in their own individual ways. This may mean, for example, that teachers should be wary of overinterpreting an experience or overmoralizing on a story. The teachers must attempt to be open to novelty emerging from the students as well as elsewhere.

At the same time, students need the opportunity to learn about and explore the knowledge and beliefs of the past and to probe some of these fully and deeply. This calls for the fine art in teaching of balancing breadth and depth, imagination and disciplined skill. A common preoccupation in recent times has been with providing freedom for students and shying away from lectures, readings, and input of any kind. These are sometimes thought to be limiting and oppressive. The suggestion here is that this input might, in fact, contribute to the students' ability to decide freely by building the students' range of knowledge and their ability to think from various perspectives.

Assumption 2. God, other persons, and the world actually enter into the life experience of each person at the intersection. Persons, then, are internally related to God, to other persons, and to the world.

Proposition 3. The person is influenced by all aspects of the environment. Persons are transformed through a myriad of external and internal events, events in the physical world, in the culture, in interpersonal relationships, and in the person's own self.

This means that physiological, chemical, and electrical processes are going on within the person all the time. At the same time the individual person is interacting within a society of other persons, ideas, physical events, and so forth. All these events form the past that is prehended by the individual. Thus, they enter into that person's experience and into the person's expectations of the future.

Educationally, this suggests a need to consider all aspects of a person's external and internal environment in planning. Persons' cognitive and affective developmental levels are important considerations, as well as their cultural context and social relationships. We need, then, to give attention to sensing where students are in their own personal concerns and ideas, to creating ethnic groupings for some educational endeavors (in which one's own ethnic culture can be explored with some seriousness and depth), to using curriculum appropriate to the development of students, to facilitating significant interpersonal experiences, to taking account of the physical environment, cultural influences, and so forth.

Proposition 4. The person at the intersection is both aware and unaware of what is going on. The individual's interaction with the many social and environmental forces is both conscious and unconscious.

Educationally, this implies that significant symbols may be quite powerful, even when they are not consciously understood. Music, visual symbols, rituals, and personal interchanges carry messages far more powerful than we may realize at first glance. We are apt to see children squirming during worship and assume that they are learning nothing, but a great deal is being communicated and received consciously or unconsciously. They are learning that this experience means something to the people around them (or that it does not), that God is somehow mysteriously present in this experience (or that God is absent), and that this community has certain beliefs about God, about Jesus Christ, and about Christian discipleship. Educators must take seriously and plan for these significant symbols as well as for the conscious and subliminal factors in the educational setting (such as the material to be presented and aspects of the physical environment). All contexts in which education takes place are settings where these factors are important. We can easily assume that visual symbols are important in worship and teacher-student relationships, in study, but this is to ignore the potency of visual symbols in the classroom and the smile across the pew in worship.

Assumption 3. The person both acts and is acted upon. These relationships at the intersection are interactive in that persons are acting upon and acted upon by both God and the world around them.

If persons are always interacting, then they are shaping the world and being shaped by it. They interact with others and with communities, with themselves and with God. Both the continuities with the past and the radical changes come out of these interactions. Persons are influenced by the social group but also contribute to preserving or changing the social patterns by what they do. Likewise, persons are acted upon and influenced by God, and God is influenced by persons and what they do and say.

Educationally, this assumption underlines the importance of considering the student as part of the educational process. One does this not just to be open or nice but because the student will interact with every aspect of the setting. By taking this seriously one can enhance the possibilities of the mutual interaction and be more genuinely open to what may come from it. This notion puts the question of openness in teaching in a broader perspective than the debate between open versus closed classrooms or permissive versus strict discipline. It protests against oversentimentalizing student-centeredness and stresses that any educational setting is interactive by nature, involving both teacher and students and both community and individuals. If either part of the interaction is underplayed, the results will be a loss in the potential learning and transformation that could emerge.

Conclusions for Educational Practice

The most general conclusion from the above is that the ability of a person or a community to integrate continuity and change can be enhanced educationally. This would involve stimulating the interactive relationship the individuals have with their environment, creating rich and varied experiences, enhancing their own reflective abilities, and stimulating novel ideas. This is the point of the theory that needs extensive mining for implications and empirical testing for effective means to accomplish the goal. The following are some initial thoughts about enhancing the integration of continuity and change in Christian education.

• modes of presentation that use or develop significant symbols for the individuals or group

• curriculum and methods that bring the historical Christian tradition to life and call attention to particular elements of it (in conjunction with discussion of how present experience relates to this past

• curriculum and methods that urge the imaginary reconstruction of the future and the thinking through of utopian and biblical visions (in conjunction with discussion of how present experience relates to this future and these ideals)

• the creation or interjection of novel ideas and experiences (e.g., through encounters with persons with radically different ideas or life experiences, through simulated experiences of different kinds of situations, or through in-depth questions beyond the superficial and obvious)

• the encouragement of students' own flights of imagination and novel ideas (e.g., through fantasy trips, artistic expression, or the creation of futuristic scenarios)

• in-depth probing into ideas that are presented or emerge (e.g., asking how ideas are related to other ideas, how they relate to persons' own inner meanings, and how they function in the society)

• emphasizing mastery of certain basic skills and knowledge and probing this knowledge in reflection and discussion

• encouragement of interaction within the group and outside, with emphasis on developing interaction skills (e.g., taking the role of the other)

• encouragement of self-reflection, with emphasis on one's inner thoughts and conflicts and the seeing of oneself from another's viewpoint

• offering practice in decision-making (e.g., through case studies or in decision situations)

• modeling how integration can take place (e.g., listening oneself to new ideas and thinking about how these might fit with, or change, the content that is being presented)

3 THE TRADITIONING

MODEL OF
EDUCATION

We began this book bemoaning the pendulum swinging between an emphasis on the historical tradition and on contemporary experience in Christian religious education. This swinging implies that we must be either past- or present-oriented, and that the future plays a minimal role in education whatever choice we make. Having recognized this dilemma, we proceeded to make the daring claim that a model of education just might be possible that would transcend the dualism between past and present and deal seriously with the future as well. The promise was made of a new educational model that would maximize the possibility of both continuity and change.

In the following three chapters this traditioning model will be described and elaborated. The reader is invited to probe, question, and experiment with the model. This is the way in which the model itself can contribute to the possibilities for continuity and change in the educational ministry of the church.

The challenge inherent in presenting this model is the same inherent in using it as a guide. Dualistic language and ideas are so deeply ingrained in the commonsense thinking of the West that any plea to transcend the continuity/dualism change is met with answers that try to balance the two poles (giving each equal time) or to counteract the overstressed pole by emphasizing the opposite one. Either answer maintains the dualism. What is being said here is far more radical than it may sound on first hearing. What is being said is that the more continuous we are with our past, the greater is the possibility for transformation. What is also being said is that the more we change, the more continuous we are with our past.

The fullness of this claim can only be understood by describing the traditioning model that emerges from it. This is the intended purpose of the remaining chapters.

A Traditioning Model of Education

What is this traditioning model of Christian religious education? We have said that the model is based on certain assumptions about the church as a traditioning community and about persons as being in process. As suggested in chapter 1, the central task in the traditioning model is to involve persons in the living Christian tradition, i.e., in traditioning. Traditioning is understood as a process by which the historical tradition is remembered and transformed as the Christian community encounters God and the world in present experience and as that community is motivated toward the future.

The term *traditioning* is easily confused with traditionalism, but the latter is not what is being proposed here. Certainly no glorification of the past or simple socialization theory of education is intended. Traditionalism and socialization imply an attempt to pass on the past intact without the vital action of reform. What is being proposed here is that to be most faithful to the Judeo-Christian tradition one must reform and be reformed. Traditioning requires passing on the past and looking toward the future, for the sake of transforming our praxis in the present. What is more, the tradition itself will be transformed as persons encounter it anew and participate in it.

Traditioning is a process by which God's gifts are received and passed on, not as a static box of things, but as dynamic life-changing events. Because God has acted in the past, many of these gifts are passed on through the historical traditions. Because God acts in the present, many of these gifts are discovered in the contemporary encounter. Because God will act in the future, many of these gifts will be experienced as promise. A traditioning model of education, then, is one in which persons are formed and transformed as they receive the historical traditions and as they encounter God and the world in the present and in future possibilities.

The traditioning model is one in which the starting point of education is persons in relation to God and the world of past, present, and future. Persons in relationship are continually receiving from God and the world and being transformed. Persons in relationship are active participants in these interactions. They are influenced, and so are God and the world.

The foundations for this traditioning model are themselves new. In chapters 3 and 4 we have looked at new perspectives on the Christian community and on the nature of persons. We have recognized that the Christian community is a traditioning community, participating in an ongoing process of traditioning that is never fixed or finished and that will continue. This in itself is a very threatening idea. Witness the persons who will not have a woman minister marry them because of the biblical injunction against women speaking out in church or because that would not be traditional. Witness the person who is angry at hearing the minister suggest in a sermon that Isaiah may have been written by three or more different people and that Isaiah I and II may have been written over a period of almost three hundred years. Both responses reveal the degree of threat inherent in recognizing that the church's tradition is emerging, rather than having been poured out in completed form during a few key periods of history.

We have also turned upside down some commonsense assumptions about human nature. We have recognized, as would proponents of a socialization model of education, that persons are indeed formed by their heritage and their community. We have recognized, as would proponents of a reconstructionist model, that persons are actors in the world, capable of critical reflection on their own community and of transforming action. We have recognized that in every moment of decision persons are influenced by past, present, and future and that their decisions will always be in some way continuous with their past and in some way transformed and unique. This again is threatening because it suggests to the individualist that persons cannot escape the formative forces outside themselves. It suggests to the isolationist that persons cannot escape the impact that their actions will have on the world and on God. Thus, we acknowledge that we as human beings are always in process, that we are always acting and acted upon.

The very large remaining question, of course, is What is the shape of this traditioning model? In this chapter the shape will be sketched, and the claims and characteristics of the model will be examined. In the final two chapters the form of the model will be elaborated in more detail. Chapter 6 deals with aims, contexts, and methods, and chapter 7 with curriculum.

The Shape of the Model

We have said that the central task in the traditioning model is to involve persons in the living Christian tradition. The two dimensions of that task are hermeneutics and transformation.

The hermeneutical dimension is the opening up of persons to their historical traditions, their present experiences, and their future hopes. These are all part of the Christian story. To engage in hermeneutics is to communicate this story, to interpret it, and to encourage others to interpret it. These interpretations are done by persons standing at the intersection and relating to many aspects of the story at one time. The influences can seem overwhelming.

The transformative dimension of the traditioning model is the synthesizing of all these influences into a decision. To engage in transformation is to encourage persons to be open to the future. The decision that takes place at the intersection re-creates the persons and the tradition.

The intersection, then, is the place where both interpretation and transformation are happening. Neither can happen without the other. People will be transformed as they interpret the various parts of the story and will engage in interpretation when they experience transformation.

The Heart of the Matter

We have recognized in chapter 3 that the traditioning community is an interpreting and transforming community. The unity of hermeneutics and transformation is at the heart of this traditioning model of education. Only as we see the inseparability of these tasks do we see how continuity and change require each other. The tendency to dichotomize continuity and change will seem unthinkable if we recognize that the hermeneutical and transformative dimensions of Christian religious education cannot be pulled apart.

Imagine persons at intersections. Some intersections will be crowded and loud, while others may seem deserted and quiet. Whatever the intersection, the persons entering there will be confronted with many influences to interpret, and these influences will be transformative. They may be from within the persons or from without, but the very act of interpreting the influences will be transformative. We know, for example, that as oppressed persons interpret the social forces that keep them oppressed their responses are transformed.

What does an intersection really look like? Let us review the story of Jonah.

Once upon a time, the Word of the Lord came to Jonah. The Lord said to Jonah to go to the city of Nineveh and speak out against it for its wickedness. Jonah responded by fleeing from God's presence. He sought out a ship headed for Tarshish and went aboard.

Now a terrible storm began, and everyone on board the ship became frightened—everyone but Jonah, that is. He was inside the ship fast asleep. His sleep was interrupted by the captain who thought a prayer from Jonah to his God might calm the storm. Then someone had the idea of casting lots to see whose evil was causing the storm. The lot naturally fell to Jonah, whose fate then was to be thrown into the sea.

In the next scene Jonah was in the belly of a great fish and was lifting up a psalm of thanksgiving. After three days and nights, the Lord spoke to the fish who promptly vomited Jonah onto the dry land. Poor Jonah. He was not to have a moment's peace, however, for the Lord came again and told Jonah to go to Nineveh and proclaim God's message. This time Jonah went and did as he was told.

The people in Nineveh did indeed hear Jonah. They repented and turned immediately away from their evil ways. Now Jonah had done his duty, and the results were overwhelming, but Jonah was not impressed. He had spoken God's Word, and that Word had indeed trans-formed Nineveh—the great, evil, foreign city. That hardly seemed reason to celebrate for poor Jonah. He had gone to much trouble to proclaim that Nineveh would be over-thrown, only to have God reverse the rules and deliver Nineveh after all.

This is a story of intersections. Note three messages in this story. First, Jonah repeatedly found himself in the midst of an intersection. The story opens with the Word of the Lord coming to Jonah, and we have no indication that Jonah had sought that Word out. Jonah was moving into an intersection in relationship to God, whether or not he wanted to be there. God's Word was spoken, and God's command was given. Now for us to speak of the starting point of education as persons in relation to God and the world is to recognize that persons always do stand in those relationships even when they wish they could escape.

Notice also that Jonah made decisions. Jonah decided to flee to Tarshish, to sleep in the bottom of the boat, to offer to be thrown overboard in order to calm the storm, to pray to

God from the belly of the fish, to go to Nineveh and proclaim God's Word, and to declare his anger to God. At every intersection he was also confronted by his knowledge of Nineveh, his anticipation of what God and the people of Nineveh would do, and his own reluctance as a Jew to reach out to this evil Gentile city. Each time he made a decision, that decision was his own unique response to influences around him.

Notice finally that at every intersection Jonah was engaged in interpretation and transformation. He was transforming these influences into some kind of decision, even deciding at points to ignore and run away from certain of these influences. He was daring enough at some intersections to speak God's Word: in the form of a psalm as he prayed from the belly of the fish and in the form of a proclamation as he spoke to the people in Nineveh. Notice that speaking God's Word was not a conclusive ending to the story in either case. The speaking only opened him to more changing. The psalm did not restore Jonah to a comfortable, placid relationship to God, but to God's renewed command to go to Nineveh. Even the proclamation to Nineveh did not restore Jonah to a quiet, peaceful existence. God's response to Nineveh's repentance forced Jonah to confront his own prejudices against the wicked Gentile city. The "moral" of this story is simply that one dare not interpret the influences on oneself if one is not open to transformation. Likewise, one dare not be transformed and go to Nineveh if one is not willing to interpret the consequences of that change. The act of interpreting is always filled with the power to tranform, and the act of transformation always forces our reinterpretation. The more we are involved in one, the more we will be involved in the other.

Content

To understand the shape of the traditioning model, one quickly wants to know what is to be the content of education, or the texts to be interpreted. In this model the content of education is the past, present, and hoped for experience of the Christian community. The many different expressions of these are the texts to be interpreted.

Experience here is intended as a big concept. It includes the kind of sharing of immediate experience emphasized by experiential education but is much more. It includes the experience of individuals and of entire communities (local church or parish, denomination, universal church). It includes the community's experience of itself as an institution and also, of God and the world.

To say that this traditioning model has for its content the experience of the Christian community is to recognize the unity of tradition and experience. What we often call tradition is really a saga of experiences and their interpretation. The tradition is the expression through beliefs, actions, and values of what the Jewish and Christian communities have experienced in the past and are experiencing now. If tradition is the story of experiences, then the two are inseparable. Tradition cannot be bound to the past, and experience cannot be bound to the present. Experiences continue to happen, and these continue to be woven into the tradition. This view of tradition and experience involves the recognition that the Christian community is the product of its past, yes, but it is also the product of its present experience and of its future hope. The content of education must necessarily come from all three, for all three come together in the living Christian tradition.

Method

The functions of education are hermeneutics and transformation, telling and pondering on the story and transforming it. Each of these flows from the other and back again, so there is no prioritizing or ordering of function. Here we will deal with the specific methods of transmission and reflection (which are particularly related to the hermeneutical function) and transformation (which is related to the transformative function).

Transmission is communication and includes all the range of methods by which the community's beliefs, actions, and values are communicated. Transmissive methods respond to the hermeneutical question of What? What have been the experiences and ideas of the Christian community? What are they now? What is to be hoped for? Transmission, then, is not just the handing down of the past but is also the communication of the contemporary witness of faith and of future hopes. This is the telling of the story, the sharing of ideas, actions, and images that have become part of that story. It also includes the transmission of culture (e.g., knowledge of other religions, the human sciences, and so forth) for the sake of instigating a dialogue between this knowledge and the community's story. If persons hear the historical Christian story in isolation from the sociopolitical events in their world, transmission is doomed to abstraction.

Transmission can take place through the didactic methods often associated with transmissive education and also through cultural forms (such as art, liturgy, and music) normally associated with socialization models of education. We need not abandon entirely the schooling/instructional paradigm as John Westerhoff would have us do.[1] Neither do we need to expect that all the church's education will take place in the classroom. Our hope lies in the recognition of the aliveness and richness of the story as it is communicated and lived.

The educational ministry needs, then, to be enriching, communicating the various expressions, memories, and hopes of the community. The communication of these enables persons to enter into experiences other than their own and to broaden the ideas, actions, and images out of which they live.[2] This is the way persons come to have a rich story background in which they find resources for interpreting their present experience.

Ross Snyder suggests that persons seek to interpret their life experience by creating a meaningful saga that explains the events in their life. He further suggests that this creation of saga is influenced by the bigger stories that people know.[3] One can conclude, then, that the richer our story background, the greater are our resources for interpreting our immediate experience. Story means not only the biblical story but also the church's historical story and the story emerging in the church and in our globe today. The story, or saga, includes all the experiences of the Jewish-Christian community woven together into a pattern of meaning.

Education, then, is the communication of a wealth of experiences: experiences that are historical and contemporary, experiences of self and of others, experiences of passionate involvement and of action, experiences of struggling together with theological concepts and life issues, and experiences of celebration. The transmission of these forms the reservoir from which the community draws. A reservoir of community experience provides a depth out of which persons can draw models of action and insight as well as resources for giving birth to new actions and insights.

Not only does transmission provide a wealth of experience, it also provides persons with a sense of connectedness—connectedness to other people, other times, and other places. Surely the first hearers of Mark's Gospel were comforted to hear how many times Jesus' disciples had failed to understand or to act, even in the midst of their following Jesus. This is not so different from children's enjoyment of stories of their parents' mischief and mistakes. The sense of shared experience or shared humanness links persons together. For something to have meaning for us, it must be something we can connect with and, therefore, something we have learned about or experienced in some way.[4] This requires the activity of transmission.

In addition to transmission, reflection must be a prominent method in Christian religious education. The two together are particularly related to the hermeneutical function in the traditioning model. This is asking the Why? of hermeneutics, the questions of meaning. Persons ponder the past, present, and future witnesses of faith and bring these into dialogue with their own experiences, their own actions and the actions upon them. The dialogue is an inner conversation that gives rise to decision and action.

Reflection includes both the objective mode of thinking about an idea or experience and the subjective mode of thinking into that idea or experience. The former can be called critical reflection and the latter, depth reflection. This double emphasis is similar to Bernard Meland's idea that both critical inquiry and affective imagination are important to the appreciative consciousness of the human spirit.[5]

Critical reflection is stepping back from an idea or event and critiquing it from various points of view. It includes identifying and sharpening issues, perhaps even weeding out extraneous detail. Especially important to the prophetic functions of ministry is the critical examination of oneself and one's community. Depth reflection, on the other hand, is immersing oneself in an idea or event. It is living with a concept. As persons actually live with an idea, it begins to take shape in more fullness. Critical reflection is looking at two or three viewpoints on human despair, analyzing these against each other, and focusing in on particular issues. It may include looking for and analyzing the despair in oneself and one's own community. Depth reflection may be entering into the world of a person whose life is characterized by despair. Both contribute to the fullness and clarity of our understanding.

Two of the most fruitful contemporary appeals to bridge the split of present from past and future have come from Ross Snyder and Thomas Groome. Snyder appeals to a creative meeting of past, present, and future, drawing heavily from George Herbert Mead's concept of sociality.[6] Groome appeals to a critical reflection on present action in light of the historical tradition and future hope.[7] These two approaches of Snyder and Groome are amazingly similar at the heart, but the former is highly subjective while the latter is predominantly objective. Snyder does more in the depth reflection mode, and Groome in critical reflection.

Are we to hear that the meeting of past, present, and future must be dominated either by the subjective or by the objective? Is the creative, interpersonal culturing of Ross Snyder incompatible with the critical reflection of Tom Groome? Certainly persons focused on depth reflection can, and often do, reject critical reflection as irrelevant. Likewise, persons focused on critical reflection often reject depth reflection as unscientific. If personhood has both objective and subjective dimensions, however, as George Herbert Mead would suggest, then to choose between these two emphases in education is a dismal thought. Education for continuity and change needs to maximize both the subjectivity of depth reflection and the objectivity of critical reflection.

Having focused on both the transmissive and reflective aspects of the hermeneutical function, we turn now to the transformative function in Christian religious education. Through the transforming methods both the tradition and the persons within that tradition are re-created. The heritage is enlarged, and the actions of the community are transformed. Transformation is concerned with How? How is the community to act in the direction of the Kingdom of God—to be open to God's promise and to reconstruct its actions, beliefs, and values in light of its past, its present, and its hope? Transformation is initiated by God's action, but we are called to respond to God's gift and God's pull. We are called to impact the world where we are.

This message is different from that of the progressive religious educators and reconstructionists who were optimistic about the possibilities of reconstructing the world through the educational process.[8] This is more in tune with the theologians of hope who put emphasis on the idea that God calls us toward the future. Moltmann is insistent that God's kingdom will come through God's promises and not through human effort, but he emphasizes the need for human activism in the world. Moltmann asserts that the mission of the church is not only proclaiming faith and hope but also transforming life in historical reality.[9] Persons are called to move in the direction of God's promises.[10] Human effort alone may not create the Kingdom, but God's call to move in that direction is clear. This means that the transformation of persons, of societies, and of the historical tradition itself are essential to our task. We are called, and our decisions at the intersection are crucial. They are not abstractions from life but are actions that impact the world.

The potential for transformation is maximized by a wealth of transmitted knowledge and by our critical and depth reflection on that knowledge. The transmitted stories themselves have power to transform. The potential for transformation is maximized by our openness to God's Spirit moving in and around us. The methods of transformation are prophetic challenge and reform—careful rebuilding of our actions, beliefs, and values. For example, challenging persons to take seriously new knowledge about food sources, land production capability, and population sizes forces the questioning of certain traditional understandings of the human response to persons who are poor and hungry. This new knowledge challenges old images of the ministries of caring. These new images may or may not be foreign to strands in the tradition. They may emerge from the recovery of a lost strand, but they may be distinctly new.

Whatever we say about transformative methods, we must recognize that what is to be transformed is not just the ills in the secular world but also the Christian community itself. We cannot simply work at transforming society so as to reduce injustice and poverty while we perpetuate uncritically our own community's tradition. Our community's beliefs and actions may, in fact, be part of the problems. We must be open to transforming our own community as well.

Goals

The primary goals of Christian religious education inherent in this model are knowledge with understanding and the transformation of persons' actions, beliefs, and values. The goals are introduced here and will be expanded in chapter 6. Fundamental to the argument is the idea that neither goal can be met without the other, for knowledge leads to transformation and transformation to new knowledge.

Looking first at knowledge with understanding, we recognize that this is not possible without transmission and reflection, so it is often associated with those methods. Knowledge of ideas and events offers a background out of which the Christian community can live and to which it can respond. This is essential to our understanding of life, our grasping of meanings. Understanding includes both a personal and a communal grasping of meaning. Understanding, then, is the integration of knowledge into one's own perspectives and into perspectives that can be communicated and shared with others. Understanding is enhanced as new ideas and events are passed on and as the community searches for meaning in these ideas and events through depth and critical reflection.

The transformation of belief, action, and values results from new knowledge with understanding. It results also from the prophetic challenge that calls us to be transformed, to know and to do the will of God (see Rom. 12). Belief is a conviction or acceptance of something as true. Action is what we do. It is our response to the multitude of influences on us: the stories we know, the culture in which we live, and the beliefs and hopes that we hold. How are our beliefs and actions to be transformed? How are our values, our judgments of worth, to be transformed? Certainly, the possibility for transformation is opened by transmission and reflection. It is opened in our interactions with God and others. But we must always stay awake to the prophetic challenge that emerges in these events and calls us to the radical life. The transformed, radical life may be one in which old beliefs are let go, in which old actions are replaced with new, in which old values are torn down and new ones are sought. The prophetic challenge will, hopefully, help us see human pain and oppression more clearly and follow God's pull more fully. In responding to this prophetic challenge we are not only changed, but we come to new knowledge with understanding.

These two purposes, knowledge with understanding and transformation of belief and action, give some idea of how one might evaluate what is happening in educational ministry. The evaluation would be twofold: What knowledge of events and ideas has been learned, and what new insights do persons have into the meaning of these events and ideas? What changes are emerging in belief, action, and values? In order to assess the impact of education in the traditioning model, these two questions suggest the kinds of evaluation queries that might be most revealing.

Claims of the Model

Expanding this account of the traditioning model of Christian religious education involves the elaboration of the claims for the model. These claims bring the model into clearer focus and display its potential for maximizing continuity and change.

The first claim of the traditioning model is that education functions in the community to transmit tradition (both what is past and what is emerging now), to enable people to interpret the meaning of their own experience, and to open the possibility of transforming the individuals, the faith community, and the world. The functions, then, are both to conserve and to transform. This idea is easier to say than to understand because the conserving functions are often understood as antithetical to the transforming functions and vice versa.

That Christian religious education has a function in the Christian community is not usually disputed, but just what that function is may be debatable. In fact, much recent discussion has been focused more on the context of the educational ministry than on the function. This is particularly true of the advocates of socialization models of education. John Westerhoff, for example, has particularly emphasized the context of Christian education as the community of faith. He understands the means of education to be enculturation, which itself "focuses on the interactive experiences and environments within which persons act to acquire, sustain, change, and transmit their understandings and ways."[11] If the context is the dominant influence on education, then what is going to broaden the visions of persons in a given context beyond their own immediate belief, values and action? What is going to contribute to the changing that Westerhoff mentions? Concern for function needs to be renewed and brought back to a place of prominence.

The second claim for this model is that education can be designed to maximize both continuity and change and their integration. Since interpretation and transformation are both functions of education in the faith community, the task of education is to accomplish each fully. The claim involves the denial of inverse relationship between continuity and change. The increase of one does not necessarily mean the decrease of the other. The claim is that the maximizing of continuity contributes to the maximizing of potential for change when the integration of the two is also maximized. After all, the more a community knows and understands of its past, the more options it has to draw from in its present transformations. Likewise, the maximizing of change contributes to the maximizing of potential for continuity when the integrative tasks are done well. When a community breaks an old pattern and changes its actions, it does so with a heightened sense of the historical tradition, of the old pattern. Only when persons are confronted with novelty do they really become conscious of the traditional patterns out of which they live. At this point the change has heightened a sense of their continuity with the past, and the community has the option to choose the old or the new. Whichever choice is made at this point, it is made with consciousness of the other possibility. The apparent contradiction of this claim will be developed further below.

The third claim is that the traditioning task is most fully engaged when the elements of past, present, and future are brought into continually new decisions. Note that the suggestion is not for a simple adding up or balancing among these three foci. The suggestion is closer to the dialectical relationship Thomas Groome has suggested in his present dialectical hermeneutics.[12] Groome has called educators to heed the importance of keeping both the past and present in continuing dialogue, and he has further stressed the often ignored concern for the future. Similarly, Dwayne Huebner has urged educators to recognize human temporality and the impact of past and future on the present.[13] The suggestion here is quite compatible with Groome and Huebner but is pushing toward an additional emphasis. The suggestion here is that the past, present, and future stand not simply in dialectical relationship or in creative tension but also in an internal relationship in which they are continually producing new syntheses, new forms. The past and future not only stand in dialectical relationship with the present but actually become part of the present. The past story, present context, and future hopes become part of the immediate experience so that the immediate experience actually incorporates them into itself.

This means that all these factors influence how we respond in the present and how we interpret the meaning of our life events. For example, the story of the prodigal son was told several hundred years ago, but a person in the twentieth century may find that the story influences his or her response in a given situation and his or her interpretation of the meaning of that event. That parable actually becomes part of the present event and the person's interpretation of it. The parable is an objective element of the past told in a particular time and place and retold in other times and places and points toward God's future. The parable also has a subjective involvement in the present. Education has a role in uncovering the meaning of that parable in other times and places through critical reflection on all available sources. This involves communicating and reflecting on the work of scholars and other interpreters. Education also has a role in promoting persons' subjective engagement of the parable and their consciousness of its role in their thinking and doing. The task of the educator, then, is to open gateways so that persons may hear the story and be influenced by it.

The fourth claim of the traditioning model of education is that the traditioning task takes place for persons in a particular time and place. The various texts are brought into focus for persons in a particular time and place through the process of hermeneutics. The texts are the different expressions of the community's past, present, and hoped-for experience. They are not only the texts of the Bible or historical tradition but also the texts emerging from the contemporary world and from persons' hopes for the future. The texts include also the novelty that emerges through the work of God's Spirit in the present moment. The interpretive process, then, is a bridge that links persons with what has gone before, with the sociocultural factors in the present, with the promises of the future, and with the novelty that emerges from the uniqueness of the situation and from the mysterious workings of God. These come together, and we make a decision. These factors are transformed by, and transformative of, the persons in this particular time and place.

Thus, when persons act their decision to act is influenced by their own past experience, by the context in which they live, by their own expectation of the future, and by God's action toward them. The decision, or act, that results will be the unique union of all these factors at a particular time and place in history within a particular person or community. This combination, or synthesis, will be new and creative but will not be totally different from early syntheses, for these earlier unions are part of it. Though this new synthesis is creative and includes the past, it will not replace the past. New generations will need access not only to these new syntheses but also to those that have gone before. Just as in biblical studies the discovery of an ancient manuscript sheds light on later manuscripts, the contemporary process of traditioning does not replace the tradition of the past but must continually rediscover it.

A fifth claim for the model is that Christian religious

education is both personal and interactive, taking place as people enter into each other's life and into relationship with God and the world of past, present, and future. As noted in chapter 4, the ability of a person or community to integrate continuity and change can be enhanced educationally. One important element in that is enhancing the interactive relationship individuals have within themselves and with their environment. Persons are by nature related: they are internally related to God, to other persons, and to the world. These relationships become part of persons' experience and enter into their personal decision and transformation. The depth and richness of these relationships, then, is very important. This calls for the kind of interpersonal educational ministry that is central for Paul Irwin, Martin Lang, and others.[14]

Further, interaction is what makes traditioning possible. Traditioning is an ongoing function of the Christian community, which means that it is a concrete task involving real persons and events. The fact that the task is influenced by past and present events and by future expectations suggests that traditioning involves interaction and synthesis of these various influences.

As persons interact with their own past, present, and future and with those of others, interpretation and transformation are made possible. The greater the interaction, the more richness is possible in the interpretation, and the greater is the potential for transformation. This means that the traditioning task requires a wealth of relating among persons, among cultures, and among epochs of history. Ross Snyder suggests that this kind of richness in relationships leads to interconsciousness, or the ability to meet another person subject-to-subject. Essential to the traditioning task is this same kind of breadth and depth of experience. What is called for is experience that is both rich in interaction and deeply personal. This is much like Snyder's plea.

> To be interesting (and to be profitably interpersonal), we must have gone places and had considerable feelings and ideas

aroused, have interiorized interesting people until their aliveness sings in us, have at least one thing we do fairly well, one interest we really know something about, have mulled over our experiences and let our imagination create.

Without such richness, a person does not have materials with which to build inter-consciousness. Nor can he understand very well another's subjectivity.[15]

Added to Snyder's personal view of interconsciousness we must recognize the important interaction of persons with other societies and cultures as well. These interactions are essential to global interconsciousness, and through them traditioning can have meaning in a global context.

Another claim of the traditioning model of education is that since education is personal and interactive it can be significantly informed by developmental theory. One could say that the traditioning model stands on the shoulders of the developmental theories. The content, methods, and purposes of education need to be influenced in part by the psychosocial issues, the cognitive patterns, and the faith perspectives of the learners. Education must necessarily be guided by the development of those persons in whom the syntheses of past, present, and future are forming. Christian education is not so concerned with creating syntheses and passing these down as with making it possible for ever-new syntheses to be formed. This requires teachers to be aware of the learners: their issues, their modes of thinking, and their faith perspectives. Developmental research and theory offer a wealth of insight into such questions. Teachers need to be deeply informed by those insights.

A related claim is that Christian religious education can be significantly informed by learning and instructional theory. Persons are influenced not only by internal developmental processes but also by the societies and environments that touch them. For this reason, the influence of the broader social and physical environment and the influence of the teacher and immediate learning environment are important for study.

Attention is given by learning theorists to the factors in the environment that lead to learning and change. Of particular interest here would be an understanding of factors in the environment that contribute to the acquisition of knowledge with understanding or to change in belief, values, and action.

Instructional theorists have given particular attention to the effect of the teaching process on students' learning and behavior. Since the teacher, as well as the students, is a part of the educational process, the functioning of the teacher must be subject for study, and the educational process must be informed by results of such study. Alfred North Whitehead has suggested that teaching should follow the natural rhythms of learning through stages of romance, precision, and generalization.[16] Students, then, would be introduced first to the glamour of a subject before moving into the more detailed and precise learning. Both of these precede the student's learning to generalize on the subject. Also concerned with instruction is Jerome Bruner, who has done considerable research on the impact of different modes of presentation on learning.[17]

James Michael Lee keeps this need for instructional theory in the forefront of discussion in Christian religious education. He urges that this teaching process inform our work as well as the learning process.[18] The recognition of the importance of learning and instructional theories in the formulations of Christian religious education is a recognition that the shape of education is influenced by the teaching-learning process itself. The process of education influences the outcome.

Characteristics of the Traditioning Model

The traditioning model of education should have certain characteristics that reveal its dynamic character. The hope would be that the educational process would be marked by at least these four characteristics.

Dialogue

The traditioning model is by its nature dialogical, opening up dialogue between persons, between cultural groups, within persons, and so forth. In these interactions both hermeneutics and transformation take place.

Hermeneutics requires the communication of various kinds of texts and the interpretation of these texts. This calls for the kind of transmission and reflection discussed above. The reflection is really a dialogue between the interpreter and the text. This dialogue could take the form of critical reflection or of depth reflection. The dialogue could take the form, for example, of the interpreter's viewing a painting and proceeding with the question-asking and analysis of critical reflection. What was the intended purpose of this painting? What does it share in common with other paintings by the same artist during the same period? How would it have been viewed by persons of that period? What is its style, and what were the artists's techniques? The dialogue may also take the form of depth reflection. How do I respond to this artistic expression? Why? How must I be like the persons for whom the painting was intended? What images are called up out of my own experience?

Transformation, likewise, takes place through dialogue. Persons are actually formed in interaction with other persons and texts. How often an encounter with another person or a particular story or film makes a lasting impression or becomes part of our store of meanings without our even knowing it. We may even be surprised to recall at some crucial moment a particular parable or psalm or experience. The interactions we have with texts and with persons become part of us, forming and transforming us, often in unexpected ways.

Curiosity and Creativity

Hopefully the education process will also stimulate curiosity and creativity. Hopefully persons will be inspired both to seek and to invent. Burning questions, exciting ideas, problems to be solved, new inventions, and dreams to be sought are all important ingredients in education.

In this task of stimulating curiosity and creativity, nothing can be more important than arousing questions. Lewis Sherrill describes the Jewish education of the first century B.C. and afterward. He notes that the emphasis in secondary education was placed both on persons' becoming thoroughly familiar with the Torah and the Mishnah and on their learning to ask good questions and to probe and interpret Scripture in light of contemporary knowledge.[19] Likewise Sherrill also notes the dynamic and questioning quality of the Hebrew education in the period prior to the destruction of Jerusalem in 586 B.C. The teaching was done in this period by parents, prophets, priests, sages, and poets.[20] Two examples serve to illustrate the vitality of the education that resulted. First, the priests and prophets were not always in agreement in their primary emphases. The priests taught through the rituals of worship, focusing on how persons approach God and on Israel's position as God's chosen people. The prophets taught through the interpretation of inner illumination and ordinary experience. They focused on God's seeking out persons wherever they are and on God's purposes, which go even beyond Israel. These different foci of the priests and prophets were inevitably in tension at times. Conflict was thus encouraged in the education of ordinary persons, and this was seen as part of the religious life.[21] Likewise, questioning was aroused in the education that took place in the home. Not only were parents models and teachers of oral tradition and upholders of discipline (including the religious codes), but they also led certain religious rites in the family. In these roles the parents not only taught and led the ritual celebrations but also had to answer their children's questions about why we do this or believe that.[22] One can see that, in both the larger community and in the home, questioning and curiosity were built into the structure. Sherrill thought that the resultant education exhibited both continuity and change. He called this one of the rarest of combinations.[23] Through early education given in informal fashion within the family, it led to emotional stability in religion. But by constant stirring up of adult thought in regard to that same religion, it not only encouraged stability but also compelled the growth of ideas within the religion.[24]

Curiosity and creativity issue out of questioning and also out of interest. One of Alfred North Whitehead's famous epithets is that "it is more important that a proposition be interesting than that it be true."[25] He added, "The importance of truth is, that it adds to interest."[26] Certainly interest must play a large part in the educational process. Winston Churchill described the dawning of his own enthusiasm for learning, a dawning that emerged in his twenties. One part of his story is particularly telling here.

> Then there was history. I had always liked history at school. But there we were given only the dullest, driest pemmicanized forms like *The Student's Hume*. Once I had a hundred pages of *The Student's Hume* as a holiday task. Quite unexpectedly, before I went back to school, my father set out to examine me upon it. The period was Charles I. He asked me about the Grand Remonstrance; what did I know about that? I said that in the end the Parliament beat the King and cut his head off. This seemed to me the grandest remonstrance imaginable. It was no good. "Here," said my father, "is a grave parliamentary question affecting the whole structure of our constitutional history, lying near the centre of the task you have been set, and you do not in the slightest degree appreciate the issues involved." I was puzzled by his concern; I could not see at the time why it should matter so much. Now I wanted to know more about it.
>
> So I resolved to read history, philosophy, economics, and things like that; and I wrote to my mother asking for such books as I had heard of on these topics.[27]

Interest was aroused when the connections were suggested between a school assignment and the living experience of a people. Interest was aroused for Winston Churchill by his own impassioned father, and that led him into further study of history. This study would itself affect the course of history.

Awe and Hope

Not only will the education process stimulate the curiosity and creativity of the students and teachers, it will also point these persons beyond themselves. It will stimulate awe and hope, i.e., a sense of wonder before these mysteries of life and a hopefulness for the future. This is a hope for the Kingdom of God, even when the signs of the times are dismal. This is not a naïve optimism that everything will always get bigger and better or that human persons will not destroy the earth by war or by stripping away the earth's resources. This hope is an awareness of the transcendent quality of life—of God's presence in, under, and over creation and of creation's ever-new possibilities. This is the kind of faith that was Abraham's as God's promise of descendants was repeated again and again and still no heir appeared. The Promised Land was struck by famine, and Abram and Sarai had to flee to Egypt. Even on their return, the promised descendants seemed nowhere in the future. God was persistent in seeking them out, even when their actions were far from deserving. They raised questions, but still they kept hoping.

Philip Phenix urges that the dynamics of the education process include hope, creativity, awareness, faithful doubt, wonder, and reverence. He believes that all these issue from the transcendent quality of persons. These dynamics spark the motivation to learn and create and question and risk, to open self to other persons and other ideas, and to stand in gratefulness and awe before life with openness to new possibilities.[28] Phenix's dynamics closely resemble what is being suggested here as characteristics of the education process, particularly as we speak of awe and hope.

The encouragement of awe and hope is no more to be equated with optimism in human accomplishment than are Phenix's dynamics. In fact, Phenix is quite critical of hope rooted in finite structures or accomplishments. Phenix speaks of human consciousness as both finite and infinite by nature. He understands sin to be persons' escaping from the infinite by immersing themselves in the finite.[29] "The denial of spirituality in the name of individual self-sufficiency or various forms of absolutism, of institution, race, class, nation, tradition, or doctrine, is evidence of this flight from transcendence."[30] The infinite is not easily defined and coded, but we will venture here to name it. The infinite is what goes beyond the limits of concrete reality. It is the transcendent quality of life that is marked by the self's transcending self, the community's transcending itself, and God's continuing promises and pull of creation toward a new future. Persons stand before the infinite, and one hopes that Christian religious education will stir their awareness of the "hoped for but not yet." One hopes that genuine awe and hope will be inspired.

Integration of Thought, Feeling, and Action

The debates among cognitive-, affective-, and action-oriented education models have worn thin by now, but they continue. The mark of traditioning education is that persons are formed and transformed in all these dimensions of existence. The separation of thought from feeling and action is artificial anyway, in that change in one of these will inevitably lead to change in the others. When only one is chosen as the target of the educational process, all three suffer.

The integration of thought, feeling, and action is inspired when education is designed with some attention to all three. When education is defined purely in terms of the quantity of knowledge taught or the expression of feelings or behavioral objectives, something is lost. The quality of knowledge taught tells us nothing about persons' own reactions to that knowledge and incorporation of it. The expression of feelings tells us nothing about the deeper transformations that are taking place and are both rooted and reflected in knowledge and action. Behavioral objectives, focused on certain patterns of behavior, inevitably omit some patterns that may also be quite important. Further, behavioral objectives are limited to those transformations that can be observed and measured, ignoring, for the most part, the qualities of inner life that are inaccessible to behavioral measures.

The traditioning model of education is built on serious consideration of all three dimensions: thought, feeling, and action. All three are nurtured, informed, and reflected on. As these are continually integrated in the education process, persons are indeed transformed.

All these claims and characteristics of the traditioning model of education remind us that persons do stand at the intersection with influences from all directions. The purpose of education is to facilitate persons' creative responding to all these influences on them. What is being called for is a traditioning process that opens up the worlds of past, present, and future and evokes inspiration and courage to enter fully into a living tradition. To enter into that tradition, one bears responsibility for taking seriously the historical tradition and future hope. Further, one risks being transformed and being called to transform the world.

Reformulation of Education Practice

What does Christian religious education look like in a traditioning model? We have noted that the traditioning model is one in which the starting point of education is the person or group in relation to God and the world of past, present, and future. The persons are not just Johnny, Maria, Bill, and Claudette who have certain needs, abilities, and interests. They are also persons who are in relationship with God, with significant others, with a variety of social groups and cultural symbols, and with a physical environment.

Let us look at Johnny, Maria, Bill, and Claudette, for example. Johnny is a child who knows only one kind of life-style, whose parents are rearing him to take over the family business. They want very much for the school, church, and community to express and reinforce the values that they hold. Maria is a child whose parents have emigrated from Mexico and who feels much more comfortable with other persons from Mexico than with the variety of persons in this church behind her house. Bill is a child with a learning disability. He is teased by the children in his neighborhood and basically ignored by the adults and children in the church. Claudette is a child who is very confused about religion. Her father is Roman Catholic, and her mother is Jewish. A neighbor has been bringing her to visit this Protestant church, but it does not make much sense to her. She does have an active prayer life. She speaks to God about her confusion, not daring to discuss it with anyone else.

The traditioning model of education calls attention to the

need to be sensitive not only to the uniqueness of each of these people but to the way in which each participates actively in the living stream of tradition. These children are not unusual. Most persons will be able to identify Marias and Bills in their own life experience. These Marias and Bills may have other names, or they may be adults instead of children. Each one is in relationship with God and the world. They are continually being acted upon, and they are continually acting and reacting. They are continually being transformed, and they are transforming. These interactions need to be the focal point of the education process, for this is where traditioning takes place.

In our group of four children the teacher's role may be primarily to create openings for them to hear and see more of their own family traditions and of the cultures from which these spring. The teacher's role is to create openings for the sharing of these stories, for the telling of stories from the historical Christian tradition, and for the telling of stories from contemporary cultures. The teacher's role is to create opportunities for interpreting these stories in light of each other and in light of the Christian hope for the future. The challenge is to create an environment that facilitates the children's reflections and synthesis of these various stories so that the stories can enter fully into their own experience. The teachers's role is to facilitate culture-making out of the interactions of this group with each other and with the past and future that they explore. *Culture-making* is just another word for tradition-forming. It takes place as persons create new relationships, new art forms, new music, new stories. Culture is not made out of pure novelty but out of the past, present, and future as these come together with novelty in the group of people who are creating.

Aims: What Is to Happen?

Though much concern has been raised in recent years about the total identification of education with goals and learning,[1] we cannot avoid these questions altogether. The very concept of education suggests that some person or persons have aims for others. Whether we talk about inductive education that draws out the insights present within persons or deductive education that communicates insights to persons, we are referring to a process that has an aim, that involves learning in some form, and that involves an agent or facilitator or teacher.

The problems arise when aims are so ambiguous and vague as to mean nothing, when they are so specific and concrete as to point to nothing beyond themselves, when they are not harmonious with the educational methods, when they do not relate to the students' own goals in any way, or when they are taken to be the whole of the educational process, leaving no opening for the novel or the transcendent.

Exploring the aims of the traditioning model provides a way to describe the model and to see what hopes underlie it. The aims of education are what education points toward or leads to. The aims implied in the traditioning model grow out of the shared life of the group as it is enlarged and enriched by the group's individuals and by the larger community of faith. Both the individuals and the larger community bring tradition and accumulated experience to the situation, and these inform the aims. This means that the aims are both internal and external. They come from within the group of Maria, Claudette, Bill, Johnny and their teacher. They also come from the congregation or parish in which this group exists, and they come from the denomination or connectional church bodies that suggest what may be important in the educational process of this group.

This view of aims is radically different from that of John Dewey, R. S. Peters, and other empiricists who have given attention to the philosophy of education. Dewey and Peters both argue strongly against externally imposed aims in favor of aims that grow out of the immediate situation.[2] They would likely have no objection to much of what I say here, but the suggestion that some aims might come from persons and groups and ideas outside the immediate educational setting would likely raise some questions for them.

The view that nothing in education should be imposed from outside the group is a view that still has influence. It has led many to reject the idea of denominational curriculum altogether in favor of purely indiginized forms of education. The trend has been toward curriculum that is homegrown within one's own congregational or parish setting. Walter Vernon refers to this trend as the "era of localism."[3] But in the traditioning model the focus is on the educational group in relation to all these outside forces (congregation, connectional church, subcultures in the larger society, and so forth). The group is not isolated. Therefore, the education that takes place in this group cannot ignore the influences from without any more than it can ignore those from within.

At the same time, the aims of education must not be purely external but need to be flexible and responsive to the situation. This means that the aims need to be open for ongoing revision. They need to be part of the educational process itself, to closely relate to methods, and to generate reformulations of aims and methods. In this emphasis the proposal here bears much in common with Dewey's understanding.

About Ideals (Visions), Goals, and Objectives

For several years a central emphasis in education has been on goals and objectives, with occasional mention of something more grandiose called ideals. So far in this chapter these terms have been avoided by keeping the discussion to aims. The concept of aims offers a generic word that describes the direction toward which the education process points or leads. That concept becomes more useful when we distinguish among different kinds of aims: objectives, goals, and visions.[4]

Objectives are simple, concrete, and attainable aims. They are the most basic empirical ends that are aimed for and that lead then to the formation of new objectives. They are the particular hopes for particular situations. An objective for our group might be learning to sing a popular Mexican hymn.

Goals are general hopes that are really complex patterns of objectives valued by a person or a group. The objective of learning to sing the hymn in Spanish might be one small part of a goal that the whole group gain more understanding of and appreciation for expressions of faith in different cultures, particularly in those most directly associated with the persons in the group. The goal in this case influences the objectives that are chosen, but the outcomes of the objectives may also lead to reformulation of the goal. The goal of understanding and appreciation is more general and less clearly measurable and attainable than the objective of learning the hymn. However, the goal points beyond the particular objective to the broader aims of the educational process. Though broad, these goals need not be so vague as to be nondescript. They need to be always stated as clearly as possible and open to reexamination and change.

Ideals are the eschatological hopes of the Christian community, the hopes about ultimate things. But we speak here of visions rather than ideals in order to convey the dynamic, transcendent nature of these eschatological hopes. These are the prophetic visions that call us beyond where we are. They are no more static, or fixed, than the objectives and goals. While they inform the choices and reformulation of goals and objectives, the visions themselves are being transformed as persons and groups proceed in aiming at their objectives and goals and reflecting on the outcomes. The vision of the unity of the Christian community may be underlying the objective and goal discussed above. The process of educating, however, may unfold new objectives and goals, and these may lead to reflection and revision of the vision.

In our example, the teacher may find that teaching the Mexican hymn in Spanish does not lead to the intended goal because three of the children express anger about how hard this is to learn. Maria feels embarrassed, then, rather than appreciated for her Hispanic culture. This failure may lead to a revision of the educational objectives—perhaps a visit to a Spanish-speaking church or a visit from an Hispanic musical group. The educational goal may then be revised to include not only understanding and appreciation of faith expressions in various cultures but also understanding of one's own resistances to faith expressions that seem foreign to one's own experience. The vision may also be revised from the unity of all Christians to the unity of all Christians in their diversity. This kind of revision of objectives, goals, and visions is, in fact, what many teachers already do, whether or not they are conscious of it. The consciousness of the processs can simply make it more helpful to one's work of deciding what to do and how to do it.

The boundaries among objectives, goals, and visions may not always be clear-cut. One objective, for example, may be related to two overlapping goals. The purpose of this delineation is simply to bring some coherence and usability to the concepts.

Visions, Goals, and Objectives in the Traditioning Model

Now, what is the unique character of visions, goals, and objectives in the traditioning model of Christian education? These cannot be defined in static terms lest they contradict the very nature of the model. The model does suggest, however, something about the character of these aims.

Objectives. The objectives in this model would be synthesizing, transforming events. Surely an infinite variety of such events could emerge. The focus of these would be on engaging persons in the Christian tradition and on the creative decisions they make as they relate to God and the world. The objectives then would be stated in terms of transforming events in which engagement and decision are facilitated. For example, one objective might be that persons would discuss the similarities and differences in the election of leaders in the biblical times of the judges and kings, in the Middle Ages, in the Reformation, and in the present time in their own country. Another objective might be that persons examine their own priorities in terms of how they use their time during a typical week and that they critique and revise these priorities in light of their vision of the Kingdom of God and the expectations communicated by their culture and their faith community.

Goals. The goals in this model have been alluded to in chapter 5. We barely scratched the surface there when we said that the goals are knowledge with understanding and transformation. These seem like very ordinary goals indeed, but the combination is not ordinary at all. Learning facts is often assumed to run counter to understanding or insight and, even more so, to transformation. How many times do we hear "head knowledge" used pejoratively while preference is expressed for "understanding in the heart"? When a professor brings out lecture notes, students often moan at the possibility of a dull session irrelevant to their real concerns. And students of all ages often complain about didactic forms of education in the church. Theorists such as Paulo Freire criticize "banking" methods of education (which store up knowledge in students) as being alien to humanizing methods.[5] And John Westerhoff calls for the discarding of the schooling/instructional paradigm in Christian education. He sees this paradigm as appropriate for teaching knowledge about religion but not for producing faith.[6]

All this is to say that the prevalent tendency in education is to separate knowledge, understanding, and transformation into independent, and often contradictory, aims of education. This tendency is not without merit, for knowledge that does not contribute to understanding and transformation can indeed be dehumanizing. Likewise, knowledge about religion can be empty without the transformation of persons' faith.

On the other hand, what kind of humanization and faith development can take place without the enrichment of persons via knowledge of their own history and of cultures across the globe. This is not to suggest that the more knowledge persons have, the more humanized and transformed they will be. This is to suggest that an increase in knowledge can increase the possibility of understanding and transformation. Knowledge with understanding and transformation, then, are not two separate and distinct goals of education. In the traditioning model these goals will be interwoven in many patterns. Knowledge with understanding and transformation are so inextricably bound that they cannot be separated as aims of education. An increase in one inevitably increases the possibilities that the other will also increase.

One can see this relation in many events of ordinary experience. When persons learn more facts about Judaism and Christianity and their relationship in history, they usually come to a greater understanding of the bonds and differences between the two religions. When persons visit Hawaii and understand something of the diversity of its people and the intermingling of cultures there, they often seek out facts about the different migrations of people to the islands and the characteristics of the various cultures that these people brought with them. When people are transformed, when they change in their beliefs or actions, they usually pursue new knowledge and understanding with great curiosity. When they reject a particular idea about God, for example, they often actively seek new knowledge and understanding of God. When they experience some form of conversion, they often study eagerly for more knowledge and understanding of their change. Lewis Sherrill points to the transformation of life-meaning that comes from encounter with the Bible.[7] Likewise, an increase in understanding or transformation can increase the possibility of a person's seeking new knowledge of the Bible and tradition.

Visions. Three visions that are particularly suggested in this traditioning model of education are the visions of keeping

faith alive and open to transformation, of fostering relatedness with God and with human persons, and of pointing
toward the Kingdom of God. These are not visions that the
community can optimistically hope to realize, even through its
best efforts. These are visions, rather, that highlight the
communty's dependence on God and put communal efforts
into the much larger perspective of God's work. Other visions
will emerge as people travel together on the journey of faith.
The very act of visioning keeps the community open to the
future as well as subject to being judged inadequate in light of
the future hopes. A congregation, for example, that uses all its
energies in helping individuals feel good about themselves,
might glimpse a larger vision and recognize that they are
ignoring relationships with larger communities and with
oppressed people of the world.

The tension between the empirical objectives and the
visionary ideals is not new for the Jewish and Christian
communities. These communities have historically lived
between the call to concrete decision and action in everyday
life and the call to an eschatological vision. Christian
educators cannot expect to escape this tension. They cannot
just vaguely state grandiose visions to justify their work.
Neither can they boil all their work down to a handful of
concrete and manageable objectives. The fact is that Maria,
Johnny, Bill, and Claudette must be addressed in some real
and concrete ways next week. That concrete address,
however, is a participation in a living tradition that is called
forward toward God's future.

Contexts: Where Does Education Take Place?

Much ado has been made over the settings or contexts of
education in recent years. Some educators have chosen to
multiply the number of possible settings so that the list grows
with each new experiment. Others have chosen to eliminate
the distinctions and speak of only one broad context, e.g., the
community of faith. In either case, optimism prevails. The

resolution of the context is taken to be a central question (if not the central question) for the reformulation of Christian religious education.

On the one hand, the attention to the educational context seems out of proportion to its importance. We hear John Westerhoff's convincing plea that the context needs to be shifted from the Sunday school to the community of faith.[8] This shift is presented as a remedy to our present dilemma as if the problems accompanying the Sunday school would not exist if the Sunday school were eliminated and replaced by the community of faith. The rethinking of the context does indeed shake the foundations and lead to healthy critique of educational systems. It does, however, leave many unanswered questions, and many people in educational ministry are perplexed, wondering what they should be doing. The context debate, as presently framed, leaves open the larger questions of the nature of the Christian community and the related questions of the function of education in that community. The goals and methods of Christian religious education are also left untouched. The changing of particular contexts, then, does not seem to be a panacea for all the ills of the church's education.

A case in point is the shift in many Protestant denominations from a director or minister of education to a director or minister of program. This is taking place with little consideration of the meaning of the word *program,* which is thought to be more comprehensive than *education* and certainly does suggest a reaching into all the settings of the church's ministry. The problem is that *program* may be narrower in its connotations than *education. Program* is suggestive of planned activities or events but bears no reference to their function. Education may include such programs, but it may also include person-to-person dialogue, individual study and reflection, and any number of functions that do not fit neatly under the program umbrella. The word *program* emerges when we define education in terms of context, in this case, the program settings of the church. This context may be broader than what is often thought of as the context of education, but this shift leaves the question of the function of education in the community virtually untouched. The question of context is given top billing to the neglect of other questions.

On the other hand, the attention to the educational context seems to be underplayed. Perhaps we have not yet taken seriously what it would mean to reflect critically on the context of Christian religious education. Malcolm Warford argues that the context is crucial but does not suggest that a simple shift of educational settings will alleviate the education dilemmas. He calls instead for a radical critique of the whole church structure, including the structures of education.[9] This would lead to the emergence of new contexts more liberating than the present ones. Warford does not suggest, however, what those new structures might be. In fact, he sees the revision of the context as an ongoing process that involves continued examination and reformulation of the church's ethos.[10] This kind of reformulation is not done once and for all but at particular times and places, at particular times in history and in particular churches or congregations.

Whatever else can be said of the context of Christian religious education, one can certainly recognize that it has emerged as a focal issue in contemporary discussions. Unfortunately the discussion has sometimes attended considerably more to what the particular contexts are than to their relationship to the large context of the Christian faith community or the educational functions.

In a traditioning model of Christian religious education the broad context is taken to be the Christian faith community of past, present, and future with all its beliefs, values, and actions. That community has acted and been acted upon by God and the world so that it is not a context isolated from others but is deeply penetrated by God and the world throughout history and in the present and future. The function of educational ministry is to engage persons in full participation in the living Christian tradition, in traditioning. This includes engaging persons in dialogue with the tradition's past, present, and future and opening possibilities for the transformation of individuals and culture. This broad context of the Christian faith community and this traditioning function need to influence what the particular contexts, or settings, of educational ministry will be.

The particular contexts for Christian religious education are basically those in which persons are opened to their experience of God and the world of past, present, and future and are transformed. This indeed broadens the context to all areas of life, but not without the qualification of particular. The contexts are very particular: families, fellowship groups, study classes, action groups, worship services, and so forth. The particular contexts may be different, however, in the twenty-first century. We need to continually examine the Christian faith community with its heritage, contemporary challenges, and future hopes so we can continually critique and revise our understanding of the particular contexts.

Rather than list settings, we will here examine some qualifying descriptions of the contexts of Christian religious education. Four such descriptions are proposed.

Wherever Persons Seek to Be Related to the Christian Tradition

Christian religious education takes place wherever persons wonder and where they are informed in their faith and related to the Christian tradition of past, present, and future. This includes all those settings in which persons seek after meaning and in which they can be encouraged in their seeking and interpreting. These are the settings where disciplined study can be brought together with imaginative flights into a world of "once upon a time" or "I wish I may, I wish I might." These are the settings where students can learn what three different scholars have said about the story of the lost sheep and imagine what story they would tell to a group of Pharisees today. These are the settings where the story of Martin Luther can be read and discussed in depth with careful deliberation on the social and historical dynamics of the Reformation and where students might study the dynamics of the contemporary social situation and ask what call for reform is needed today. These are the settings where people dream about the ideal world and where they study the promises of God and the eschatological visions in the Bible and in the whole of Jewish-Christian history.

In short, the actions related to seeking and participating in the Christian story are at the heart of the teaching ministry of the church. Wherever these take place is an appropriate context for Christian religious education.

Wherever Persons Communicate Faith with One Another

Flowing naturally from the first description of context is this second description, which reminds us that wherever persons come together in fellowship, Christian religious education takes place. Fellowship is where faith communication takes place. The biblical image of koinonia suggests a fellowship, or sharing community, in which persons share in the mysteries and gifts of Christ in real and concrete ways. This kind of sharing is at the heart of faith communication, the giving and receiving.

This would suggest that contexts are those settings in which persons communicate faith with one another. These are settings where tradition is shared, re-presented and re-formed. The contexts include those in which people celebrate together the gifts of Christ in ritual and symbol: in the liturgy and sacraments, in art and music, and so forth. They include contexts in which persons give verbal witness to their faith: in teaching, preaching, and testimonies of various kinds. They include contexts in which faith is reflected in action: action in the church and in the world, action with significant others, and action directed toward the larger structures of society. In short, contexts are numerous and varied: family celebrations of Advent, camping trips, art and drama groups, church school classes, worship services, action groups, fellowship groups, and so forth.

As people share with each other, they actually communicate meaning through their language and gestures. If we recognize all the gatherings of the church as faith-sharing events, then we see them as the context of Christian religious education. In these gatherings, we can encourage significant communication, whether it be jovial and lighthearted or heavy and serious.

Wherever Communion with God Is Supported and Guided

If Christian religous education deals with the formation and transformation of persons' faith, then education takes place in any context where persons are supported and guided in their communion with God. This suggests that settings of worship and spiritual guidance are contexts of education, as are retreats of various kinds.

The dilemma posed by this kind of statement is that worship, then, is sometimes assumed to take the place of other contexts. The teaching ministry becomes characterized as one of the many dimensions of worship and wholly incorporated in this context. Instead I would suggest that in the ministry of liturgy, in bringing service to God, persons are indeed formed and transformed in their faith. Therefore, worship has educational dimensions in addition to its other dimensions.

Implicit in these statements is the assumption that education is not worship and worship is not education. Their respective functions are unique. To equate the two would be to deny the richness of one or both. Though they are not the same, they do overlap so that each does exist in the other. Education takes place as we worship, and worship takes place as we teach, whether or not we plan for these in intentional ways.

Wherever People Carry on the Mission of Christ

If Christian religious education deals with the communication and interpretation of the Christian story and with the formation and transformation of persons' faith, then education takes place in any context where persons enter into that story and participate in the creating of new chapters. These are the contexts in which Johnny, Maria, Claudette, and Bill participate with others in ministry in the church and the world. The laity (*laos*) of the church are the people of God called to carry on the work of Christ in the world. The broader context of Christian religious education has been described above as the Christian faith community with all of its beliefs, values, and actions. Participation in that context suggests involvement in the action of that community. And it is an action community, reaching out wherever persons or social structures have need. Participating in the living tradition of this community inevitably involves participation in this action.

This would suggest that education takes place wherever people participate in the ministries of visiting the lonely, caring for the sick, leading in worship, raising consciousness to oppression, or liberating the oppressed and their oppressors. The possibilities are unlimited, for persons learn and are transformed as they do these things. Education is not a passive process but takes place as persons actively engage in the world: acting, reflecting, and acting again.

Needless to say, these various descriptions of the context of Christian religious education flow together. One cannot identify any particular context with only one of these descriptions. The interpersonal communication of faith is related to communion with God. Relating with the Christian tradition is tied to carrying on the mission of Christ. In any particular context of educational ministry, these will flow together in various ways. Christian religious education takes place wherever persons are opened to God and the world and are transformed.

Teaching: How Do We Do It?

You are the teacher and stand at the intersection with a group of people. What are you going to do? In chapter 5 some description of the methods of a traditioning model of education was given. Two principal methods were suggested: hermeneutics and transformation. Here we will try to describe in some concrete ways what shapes these might take in teaching.

The teacher is, first of all, acting in relationship to the students. All are part of the journey of faith and meet at the intersection. This is true whether they meet in a classroom or worship service or during a retreat or work project. This is true in settings where persons are formally identified as teachers and students and where they are not. The teaching must be relevant to these persons as they meet each other and God and the world. The teaching must also be appropriate and relevant to the aims and contexts of educational ministry. We need to keep in mind the aim of enabling persons to participate in the living Christian tradition. We need to keep in mind the context of the Christian faith community with its past, present, and future and with all its beliefs, values, and actions. If educational methods are isolated from these people and this aim and context, they become technological tools rather than meaningful functions in the community. Then Maria, Johnny, Bill, and Claudette are pushed through a meaningless system rather than educated.

Teaching in Relation to Persons at the Intersection

To teach in relation to persons at the intersection is to be aware of the issues, feelings, needs, dreams, and capabilities of those persons. One must be aware, for example, of the differences in degree and types of motivation or of emotional blocks that people bring to the intersection. One must also be aware of the different external influences on persons. For example, are persons surrounded by biblical literalism or poverty or wealth or political turmoil? All these will influence their perspectives, questions, and self-identity. This suggests the need for different forms of educational ministry for different persons.

Individual differences will also exist in the openness of persons to change. This is particularly important to note in light of the concern in this book for education that maximizes both continuity and change. Some people are very resistant to anything that seems traditional. When someone asks them to discuss a modernized phrase like "God's ever-present creative love," they are eager to begin, but if the teacher asks them to study the Apostles' or Nicene Creed, they seek ways to avoid this. They may say, "This doesn't make sense" or "This doesn't bear any resemblance to the first, modernized phrase." They may even argue that the creeds are outmoded, irrelevant, or meaningless. Teaching to facilitate both continuity and change must capture the imagination of these people so that they can find excitement and meaning in exploring the tradition. This could be through (a) story-telling, (b) re-creation of historical persons and events through stories, simulations, drama, art, or (c) tracing one theme through history, noting the continuities and changes.

On the other hand, some people are very resistant to anything that creates change. When someone proposes a new way of interpreting a scriptural passage or a new plan for the church program, they reject it immediately in favor of tradition (i.e., the tradition that they know). These people may not be particularly interested in ancient tradition, but they may be committed to preserving the tradition they have experienced or have learned in school (the one they have mastered). Teaching that facilitates both continuity and change must help these people envision beyond their own experience of tradition. It must stimulate their curiosity and their ability to risk exploring new ideas. It must help them become sensitive to their own experience and that of others, and it must help them explore the richness of the tradition. It must offer opportunities for persons to (a) express their own ideas, wishes, and feelings, (b) develop listening skills and experience other points of view through role play, simulations, and so forth (as in Mead's "taking the role of the other"), (c) imagine new possibilities of beliefs and actions for the future, (d) restate familiar tradition in new words, paraphrases, and artistic forms, and (e) look at their own actions and test these against historical tradition and future promise (as in Groome's shared praxis model).

Teaching in Relation to the Aim of Traditioning

If the primary aim in the traditioning model is to enable persons to participate in the living Christian tradition, then teaching must help persons touch the meanings in their own life and in different aspects of the tradition. Teaching must help persons make the mental connections and bring these to bear on their decision at the intersection.

This calls for transmitting a rich story heritage and encouraging both critical and depth reflection on that heritage. This also calls for helping persons see ways in which they are presently helping to form and transform the tradition. Bill, Maria, Claudette, and Johnny may need explanations of how the current beliefs, practices, and values in their church came to be. What influences within and outside the church, historical and contemporary, contributed to these beliefs, practices, and values? They may also need to become more conscious of their own contributions to that tradition by expressing and sharing their ideas with others in the community through music or drama or discussion.

Teaching in Relation to the Context of the Christian Faith Community

We have noted that the context of education is the Christian faith community. This faith community is itself impacted by its past, present, and future. These come together to make the community what it is and are expressed through the various beliefs, actions, and values. The teacher needs to address persons in that community where they are. The teaching needs also to help persons learn about, reflect on, and transform that faith community in which they participate.

This underlines the importance of the teacher's communicating in the significant symbols of the particular community in which he or she is teaching. This may mean inviting science-fiction enthusiasts to create an outer-space version of the Abraham story, taking place in the year 2050. This may mean that the teacher be immersed in the events and language of football and medicine or industry and be able to draw on these for illustrations and to reflect on them with seriousness. Even more importantly, however, this means that the teacher must understand the language of the persons he or she teaches. This is for the purpose of understanding and being understood. Paulo Freire understands language to be the way in which persons refer to reality. Therefore, teachers must be able to understand the language of the persons they address if they are to understand their world and speak language that is understandable to them.[11]

Equally important for teaching is the ability to communicate in the symbols that are, or have been, significant in Christian communities in other times or places. These are also part of the context. The avenues into discovering these symbols are vast: films, books, visits to different communities, and so forth. What is important is that the teacher immerse himself or herself into these symbols so as to sense some of their significance for the communities that hear them. These can be communicated in many ways, but however the communication is done, the teacher can help people relate to these other communities by suggesting connections between their own significant symbols and those of the other communities. For example, the architecture of a church's sanctuary is usually intentionally designed to give expression to some dimensions of faith. Teaching might involve introducing and explaining some different architectural designs and asking persons to reflect on the meaning of the design of their own church's sanctuary in light of what they have learned. Or, teaching may begin with visiting several different churches and working together with students in trying to discover the meanings of symbols discovered there.

Conclusions

This chapter began with the question, What does Christian religious education look like in the traditioning model? The answer is that it looks many different ways. No magical formulas exist for perfect education. Education is itself a process in which teachers and students participate together in the living tradition. They are living together through a series of transforming events. No event is an end in itself, but in each one persons are called forward to God's kingdom.

The educational process does point to certain visions that pull the persons forward and guide the educational process. These visions are themselves open to being transformed, but some particularly important ones are to keep faith alive and open to transformation, to foster relatedness with God and human persons, and to point toward the Kingdom of God. Also, guiding the educational process is the context itself, the faith community that relates to God and the world, that bears the tradition, and that lives toward future. Within this community persons are formed and transformed in their faith, and the community itself is transformed. Education, then, takes place wherever persons are opened to their experience of God and the world and are transformed.

Teaching is meeting students at the intersection and moving with them into the future. All this takes place within the context of the historical faith community. What do we ask of a teacher then? We ask the teacher to meet students where they are and to relate to them in significant ways. We ask the teacher to participate and enable others to participate in the living Christian tradition with all that means. And we ask the teacher to understand as deeply as possible and to help others understand and respond to the context in which they are all living.

Curriculum: What Are Our Guides?

By this time the intersection must seem like a very awesome place. The question inevitably arises: What are our guides? This is the dilemma facing anyone who would teach. This is the very dilemma that leads to the great emphasis on printed curriculum.

As with context, many people are very optimistic about the possibility of resolving educational problems through curricular revisions or changes in curricular structures. Church teachers and leaders seek out a curriculum that is different from their church's offerings in hopes of revitalizing their own teaching. Publishers seek to make their own curriculum more available, more usable, and more attractive. Educational leaders seek to train persons in the choice and use of curriculum resources. A great deal of energy goes into the revitalization of curriculum resources at all levels of the church.

This energy reflects the optimism held by many persons that solving our curriculum problems will solve our educational problems. Much optimism is expressed that including more Bible in the curriculum or offering several curriculum choices with different emphases will resolve current dilemmas. Others express pessimism in these kinds of solutions and push for eliminating denominational or centralized curriculum altogether in favor of developing homegrown curriculum. We noted this trend in chapter 6. It is reflected in the large number of local parishes writing their own curriculum. Persons in these churches are optimistic that homegrown curriculum is the hope for the future of education.

So here we stand, optimistic that an appropriate road map must exist and yet uncertain about where to find it. This road-map imagery has often been used to describe curriculum. The map serves as a guide offered by an expert to a person unfamiliar with the territory. We fail to realize, even in this imagery, that a road map is of little use without a person who is searching for something, who has some ability to read maps, and who has some idea of where he or she is presently standing. We often assume that teachers are indeed searching and proceed to put the map in their hands. Sometimes we go a step further and give a few lessons in map-reading (called curriculum utilization). If we are really astute, we even give a lesson or two in finding one's place on the map (called needs assessment). We rarely take time to ask the teacher about his or her search or the students about their search. We simply assume that the map has answers to all the questions that might be asked.

Reconceptualizing Curriculum

In this era when so many educators seek the solution to educational problems in revising, reforming, or throwing out printed curriculum, we must spend some time studying deeply this issue and reconceptualizing it. In congregations or parishes, curriculum discussions often become the focal point for discussions of educational reform, and printed curriculum is often blamed for all the ills or sought as the resolution to those ills. Teachers often attribute great power to curriculum, and such a powerful force certainly deserves considerable attention in our rethinking of education.

Both Maxine Greene and William Pinar have worked at reconceptualizing curriculum. They have called the road-map view of curriculum into question, criticizing particularly the failure of such curriculum models to address the internal dimensions of the persons involved.

Maxine Greene has called attention to the estrangement of the student from the curriculum when it is not related to the student's inner structures of meaning. She recognizes the rapidly changing social world in which "the contemporary learner is more likely than his predecessors to experience moments of strangeness, moments when the recipes he has inherited for the solution of typical problems no longer seem to work."[1] She compares this strangeness with what a stranger experiences when searching a map.[2] Translated into the context of Christian religious education, this stranger issue calls up a picture of a person standing baffled before all the knowledge that people out there somewhere think he or she should know. All the pressures pour down on this person to know more Bible, to understand the relation between God and evil, to choose an ethical response to world hunger, and so forth. All these agenda are zealously put forward, and this person stands in the intersection a stranger.

Maxine Greene sees the great need in curriculum to be one of "making connections."[3] She sees people as desiring to get oriented, or to "constitute meanings." This happens only as they see themselves as actors on the world rather than aliens, and only as they enter their own interior journey.[4] Any aloofness from the world or alienation from self only perpetuates the student's estrangement as he or she stands holding a foreign map.

A similar point is made by William Pinar, who is concerned that curriculum offer more than an external guide for a journey, however well designed and appropriate to the students that guide may be. He urges that curriculum needs to focus on the travelers' experience of the journey as well.[5] This means encouraging students to explore how they experience the journey—the new information or events. In order to do this with students, teachers must become students of themselves.[6] As teachers become more aware of their own experience of the journey—they can better teach others. To teach is to travel with, or to study with, students "with wise companionship."[7]

These kinds of arguments can be used as reasons for discarding printed curriculum resources, but they can also be used to spark a new kind of study of curriculum and a new kind of design. They can, for example, spark curriculum design that itself is open. Curriculum can be designed to encourage persons toward introspection, toward reflection with imagination and free association, and toward recognizing themselves as subjects in relation to the world presented. Curriculum, then, ceases to represent an external body of knowledge from someone or somewhere else that needs to be appropriated. It represents, instead, an opportunity to enter into knowledge, respond to it, act on it. In short, the curriculum designed in this way offers the opportunity to experience world and to form world.

In Christian religious education, then, curriculum can be envisioned that offers persons the opportunity to learn about traditions so that those persons might enter into the experience of others who created and lived them. It can encourage persons to look inward to their own experience of these traditions and to enter actively the traditioning process, forming and transforming tradition.

The Shape of the Problem

All this suggests a reframing of the curriculum issue. In the churches we have often sought to overcome the estrangement of curriculum by giving people what they say they want or by discarding curriculum resources altogether. This first alternative is dominant in the current curriculum system. Pressure groups and educational leaders in parishes put forth their wishes about the style and content of curriculum, and publishers set up marketing research to find out what people want. All this input goes into the system. Then subject matter and curricular styles are discussed in committees where compromise becomes the order of the day. Out of these committees come choices to offer two or three or four lines of curriculum, one for each interest group. Out of these committees come choices to offer several different units, each reflecting a concern of one of these groups. Out of these committees come decisions to choose writers who represent different perspectives and different interest groups as well. In short, the effort is made to make the curriculum less estranged by including something in it for everyone. If you as a teacher find yourself a stranger to the offerings this quarter, keep going and wait until next quarter when your own interests may be better represented. Or you may, instead, choose one of the other curricular options more suited to your interests.

The other alternative for curriculum reform is to discard the centralized curriculum as hopelessly estranged from the local situation. This approach is gaining wide appeal in both Christian and Jewish communities.[8] This often leads people to search through local bookstores for printed resources that are appealing to their personal preferences and alleviates much of the estrangement problem. It introduces, however, another kind of problem, a privatistic approach to teaching. People teach what is appealing to them or what they think will be appealing to their students. They ignore those signals from outside that do not suit them. They choose a map that guides them through territory already somewhat familiar. The unfamiliar goes unexplored.

Another way in which churches fill the gap when centralized curriculum is discarded is to create their own curriculum. This often leads to very creative homegrown curriculum designed for a particular parish or congregation. The attempt is made here to let the curriculum grow out of the life of the parish, and when successful this can go a very long way toward eliminating the estrangement problem.

The danger of this approach is that the curriculum may simply reflect and perpetuate the parish as it is, often not drawing in outside knowledge and perspectives and not pushing the parish to critique and transcend itself. Unfortunately, however, homegrown curriculum often does not even reflect the parish in any significant way. The curriculum is often designed by one or two persons in the church who may have no more awareness of the deep, inner searchings of the people in their parishes than the curriculum writers across the country (who do, in fact, have some relatedness and sensitivity to the persons for whom they write). Further, they may not be willing or able to design curriculum responsive to these inner searchings or to the social dynamics and issues in the community. What frequently happens in homegrown curricula is a shallow skimming across subject matter, reflecting little depth of theological study or reflection and, often, even little depth of reflection on the persons in the parish. This is not because the homegrown curriculum designers are incompetent, quite the contrary. It is because the system giving rise to homegrown curriculum resources has the same flaws as the system giving rise to centralized curriculum resources.

Disconnectedness in the Curriculum System

Both of these systems are frequently marked by compartmentalization, which works against integration. This leads to a kind of disconnectedness in which subject matter is isolated from the educational method, curricular themes are isolated from each other and from life, and curriculum makers are isolated from curriculum users.

Note how easily subject matter and method can be separated, the first kind of disconnectedness. A corporate body sponsors a consultation on curriculum design. They invite a systematic theologian to present the theological content that needs to be included. They invite a religious educator to present educational methods. They then ask curriculum makers to use those methods to communicate that content. Similarly, a local church invites a theologian to give theological input to teachers on a particular subject. An educator is then asked to develop curriculum resources (activities) for the same teachers on the same subject. The theologian and educator are not asked to work together in any way nor to consult with the teachers about what is going on in their setting. The theological input is given one day, and copies of the curriculum resources are distributed. Then the teachers are asked to proceed from there. This kind of approach is intended to bring theological insight and educational method together. Instead, it promotes compartmentalization and discourages the possibilities of integration occurring when the various groups actually deal with the chosen subject. The theological input is taken to be the subject matter, which can be prepared independently of the method (curriculum activities) and of the persons involved (teachers and students). Each of these three (subject matter, method, and persons) is seen to be independent and external to the others.

A second kind of disconnectedness characterizes the organization of curricular themes. The old issue between bible-centered and life-centered themes gets resolved by providing for both separately. The two approaches are offered in two different curriculum lines or in two different units. Hence, we may deal with both kinds of themes but not together in any integrative fashion. This reinforces the isolation of past from present and future, for we provide resources for dealing with each separately rather than together. We study Abraham, for example, and then later in the year, we study what it means to be the people of God today.

Barry Holtz recognizes this same kind of compartmentalization of curricular themes as a key problem in Jewish education. He begins by recognizing that Jews in this country live pulled between two cultures and that education has only perpetuated the split.

> Throughout history Jews have lived in a kind of creative tension with their environment—influenced by and just as surely influencing the thought of others. . . . And yet it seems to me that our Jewish schools tend to reenforce the bifurcation of cultures far more than they try to meet the challenge of integration. Instead of trying to place Jewish thought and experience in its larger context, we Jews isolate it and treat it as a kind of peculiar, hothouse flower of a culture, existing in its

own hermetically sealed environment. In doing so we pass up a marvelous opportunity.[9]

Holtz is concerned that Jewish studies become isolated in the curriculum from everything else and, then, are seen as a set-apart world of reality. One of the solutions he puts forth is an integrative curriculum in which the Jewish and non-Jewish thought would be studied together on a particular theme, such as death or evil.[10]

The third prevalent form of disconnectedness is the isolation of curriculum maker from curriculum user. By this I do not simply refer to the problem of writers' not knowing personally the people for whom they write. Whether designing centralized curriculum or curriculum for one's own parish, the curriculum maker may not be given access to, or even encouragement to be involved in, the lives of the people for whom the curriculum is intended. Neither may the curriculum maker be encouraged to design curriculum that creates paths for the curriculum users into their own life experience. The curriculum resources often, then, seem irrelevant to the life of the people who use them, isolated from the life of the church and world these people experience.

This last issue is not a new one. Wide recognition is now given to the importance of considering together material resources and the human context in which they will be used. This is a recurrent theme in the 1980 issue of *Religious Education* devoted to Curriculum in Religious Education.[11] Much stress in recent years has been placed on relating teachers to the curriculum by training them to choose and use curriculum resources and by recognizing the teachers and learners as part of the curriculum process. Mary Boys also calls attention to the social relationships (such as the political dimensions) of the curriculum process and the broadening of the contexts of curriculum issues to include all areas of the church's ministry having educational components.[12] The human context of the curriculum process is, thus, very complex. It includes the political decision-making process, the cultural and personal dimensions of the parish, the teachers and students in classrooms, and the people engaged in all facets of the ministry of the church. How can curriculum designing and resourcing be done in relation to these human contexts?

Curriculum in the Traditioning Model

What is curriculum then, and how is it to be designed? Curriculum is simply a planned course. This simple definition is suggestive of a pathway (course) over which persons travel on a journey. The curriculum in Christian religious education is a particular kind of course, a pathway on a journey of faith.

Purpose

The curriculum exists in order to provide guidance to persons on their faith journey. To repeat our metaphor, a map does just that: It is a tool that provides guidance on a journey. A map, however, is only a tool and is static. It does not change as the landscapes change or as our perspectives on those landscapes change. One needs only to study ancient and modern maps to see the vast amount of change that does occur in both the landscapes themselves and in human perceptions of those landscapes. Geography changes daily as the earth is affected by the events of nature and the acts of persons on nature. Volcanoes, earthquakes, and powerful winds and rivers leave their mark. So do people. A small mountain near our home has been almost totally eliminated by mining in the last twenty years. The map, then, is subject to constant revision. Furthermore, it alone is not helpful without the elements described above: a person who is searching for something, who has the ability to read maps, and who has some idea of where he or she is presently standing.

This metaphor of the map needs to be enlarged, then, to include the travelers themselves, the guidebook, the travel plans, and the guide who is the "wise companion."[13] This image of curriculum has been described by Herbert Kliebard as a metaphor of travel.

> The curriculum is a route over which students will travel under the leadership of an experienced guide and companion. Each traveller will be affected differently by the journey since its effect is at least as much a function of the predilections, intelligence, interests, and intent of the traveller as it is of the contours of the route. This variability is not only inevitable, but wondrous and desirable. Therefore, no effort is made to anticipate the exact nature of the effect on the traveller; but a great effort is made to plot the route so that the journey will be as rich, as fascinating, and as memorable as possible.[14]

Note that Kliebard recognizes in this metaphor the roles of teacher, traveler (who is both influenced by and influences the journey), and planned course. This image is responsive to the concerns of Greene and Pinar that persons' experience of the journey be recognized as part of the curriculum.

Content

This metaphor of travel is illuminating, but what kind of journey are we talking about? Will just any journey do? If so, then Christian religious education has as its curriculum all the journeys of life, complete with teachers, travelers, and planned courses. This does not yet define the boundaries of curriculum or explain what is uniquely Christian about this education, however.

The content of the curriculum in the traditioning model is the accumulating wisdom of the Christian community. This includes the community's tradition, which is ongoing, and its accumulating experience, which is past, present, and future. This includes its experience of itself, of God, and of the world. The accumulating wisdom of the Christian community, then, is not an in-group wisdom isolated from the world, but a wisdom that grows out of the community's life in the world. Grasping the community's wisdom requires grasping the context, the world, in which that wisdom emerged and continues to emerge.

This definition of the content of curriculum is partly influenced by Lawrence Cremin's attempt to recapture William Torrey Harris's definition of curriculum as the "accumulated wisdom of the race."[15] The difference lies in the fact that Harris' idea of curriculum (formed in the 1870s) rests on an assumption of preformed static content that is passed on to students. He refers to accumulated wisdom. In fact, Harris's understanding of education has to do with a process of enabling persons to "become privy to the accumulated wisdom of the race."[16] This certainly suggests an understanding of education and curriculum that is centered on the historical tradition. Cremin, however, recognizes the dynamic elements in Harris's understanding of curriculum.

> What if we were to go back to Harris's definition of education and consider the curriculum as the accumulated wisdom of the race, to be made available to individuals through a variety of institutions in a variety of modes? And what if we were to conceive of education as the effort to define that wisdom in the large and then assist individuals in the business of sharing it more comprehensively, more economically, more self-consciously, and more critically?[17]

This return to Harris's definition suggests that curriculum is at home in a variety of contexts. The human context of the curriculum is understood broadly, inclusive of all those settings in which education takes place. This also suggests that education has a twofold role in relation to curriculum: to define the wisdom and to plan for the sharing of it. All this is consistent with a traditioning model of education if we recognize a third role for education in relation to curriculum, i.e, to contribute new wisdom to the old. This suggests that the ongoing experience of the community contributes to the tradition and becomes part of the community's wisdom.

We can speak, then, of the accumulating wisdom of the Christian community, recognizing the dynamic nature of the wisdom. It emerges from and builds on the past but is transformed in the present as that community lives in the contemporary world and looks toward the promises of God's future.

Starting Point

The starting point of curriculum in the traditioning model is persons in relation to God and the world of past, present, and future. This suggestion moves beyond the educational debate between beginning educational events with life experience or with the Bible. It moves beyond the systematic theological debate between theological reflection's beginning with human experience or with historical tradition. The argument here is that we must begin with both, that the relationship is our starting point.

If this is the starting point, then the units of curriculum are those transforming events in which people are confronted by God and the world. People are not passive objects of these events, but they bring their own creative decision to them. Out of their decisions come new insights and actions toward God and the world. These are added to the others, thereby adding to the wisdom of the faith community. So persons stand at the intersection, confronted by God and the world and the tradition of the Christian faith community (with its past, present, and hoped-for forms). These persons will decide how to bring these elements together, and their new insights and actions will guide them and others in the next steps of the journey.

Components

What, then, are the components of the curriculum in a traditioning model? The components are the persons who are teachers and students, the subject matter, and the design and resources for bringing that subject matter and those persons into dialogue.

Persons. The persons are those who travel the journey together. The teacher is a traveling companion who acts as guide. This does not mean that the teacher controls the situation but that he or she is a wise companion. The teacher shares with those on the journey and opens avenues for fellow travelers to share with each other and to explore that accumulating wisdom that is the tradition of the Christian community.

The teacher is one who facilitates hermeneutics and transformation, who transmits, reflects, and opens channels for transformation. The teacher is one who does all of these things and enables others to do the same. So the fellow travelers on the journey are together telling stories, reflecting on those stories, and transforming and being transformed. The curriculum is actually created and re-created as these travelers enter into the course of study with their own uniqueness as human beings.

Subject matter. The subject matter is also a component of the curriculum. Much attention has been given in recent years to the students and teacher as persons and to the curriculum design and resources. Very little attention, comparatively, has been given to the subject matter. Curriculum resources are often filled with suggestions about age-level characteristics and suggested activities, but the subject matter is often provided in its barest form. In a traditioning model of education the subject matter, or accumulating wisdom, becomes very important because this is part of the tradition that bears God's gifts to humanity. God has handed over the Tradition, and people continue handing on God's gifts through their telling and reforming of the tradition. This is the unending process of traditioning. Persons cannot engage in the passing on or the re-creating if they are not involved in the subject matter, the accumulating wisdom of the Christian faith community.

If the subject matter is a component of curriculum, the curriculum resources need to make available that subject matter as well as to be informed by it in method, style, and so forth. The teacher's guide, when there is one, needs to offer rich subject matter to assist the teacher in his or her own seeking. This calls for more content than the bare essentials that might be communicated with students. This calls for something more than a simplified wording of a biblical story that can be told or read. In other words, curriculum resources need to be accompanied by background material as well as presentation material. Further, these guides need to offer questions that encourage teachers to reflect on the ongoing life of their community as they prepare to teach. We noted above that this ongoing life is also part of the subject matter.

The subject matter is not only important for the teacher in preparation but also for the students. Presentation materials need to be rich. This is not an argument for complex profusion in curriculum resources but for richness. How are people to understand the grace of God, for example, if they only hear the heroic stories of God's chosen leaders: Abraham and Sarah, Isaac and Rebecca, Jacob and Esau, Saul and David? How are we to grasp the wonder of God's love unless we recognize how God continued to seek out and use these people even when they lied, cheated, and stole? These parts of the story make it more complex and more deserving at times of an R-rating, but without the complexity of Abraham and Sarah pretending to be brother and sister in Egypt or of Jacob's tricking Esau out of his birthright the stories are dry chronologies with little sense of reality about them.

The subject matter is not finished and stable, like a block of wood. The subject matter itself is transformed as persons encounter it. These two curriculum components (the persons and subject matter) are already intertwined, even before you talk about design and resources. Persons are impacted by the accumulating wisdom in different ways, and also, the wisdom itself continues to build and change as people enter into it and it is transformed.

Design. In addition to the persons and subject matter the curriculum also includes the components of design and resources. This point is not likely to be met with surprise, as we usually begin here. These components are what we most often associate with curriculum, so now, finally, we are on very familiar ground. What do design and resources look like in a traditioning model of education?

Design is simply the environmental design that facilitates traditioning—that enables persons to participate fully in the living tradition, or the community's accumulating and emerging wisdom. This suggests that design needs to include a comprehensive plan for communicating and interpreting the historical tradition (including both the Bible and the church's history). This also suggests that the design needs to include a comprehensive plan for helping people get in touch with their own experience and that of others and with their expectations and hopes for the future. This kind of comprehensive planning is a way of creating an environment that encourages traditioning. To say that curriculum design is environmental design is to recognize that the environment actively influences persons at the same time that persons are actively influencing it. Designing the environment involves providing contexts and methods that will facilitate this influence in both directions. This is an effort, not at engineering a perfect environment, but at creating a culture out of the past and into the future. This is an effort at cocreating with God and with other people.

We have argued above that curriculum includes all the experiences that contribute to the formation of persons as well as the formal courses of study. Both dimensions, then, need to be included in the design. Lawrence Cremin has noted the tendency in general education to pull between these two, i.e., to recognize the various domains in which education takes place but to ignore all but one (usually the school).[18] The same thing happens in Christian religious education when persons like James Michael Lee focus primarily on the schooling contexts and John Westerhoff, on worship and community-life contexts. A curriculum design really needs to embody all these dimensions.

A curriculum design needs to include plans for the different contexts where persons are opened to their experience of God and the world of past, present and future and are transformed. The curriculum design needs to include plans for the methods of transmission, reflection, and transformation. This makes it possible for tradition to be shared and made. Persons learn about God and the Christian faith community and the world. Persons participate in relation to God and the faith community and the world. In other words, persons engage in tradition-taking and tradition-making, transmitting and creating a culture that communicates the gospel. This emphasis is held up by Westerhoff in his attention to the ritual and community life that bears the message. Similarly, Ross Snyder calls our attention to both the formative power of culture and the role of the community in forming culture. If the totality of the contexts and methods of Christian religious education are not to be lost, then curriculum design needs to take account of all these dimensions.

All this is to say that curriculum design is not simply a master plan of printed resources. Neither is it a plan simply for formal courses of study. It is, instead, a total plan for the life of the community. It grows out of praxes, the actions of the community and the actions on the community. These actions on the community come from forces of the past, present, and future. This means that the formers of the plan must be in touch with the community as it is and with as many as possible of the forces acting on the community. The curriculum designers need to begin their work with reflection on action. The designers need to reflect on what is the present curriculum (explicit or hidden) of the church, what are the operative values, and what are the forces acting on the church (from the past, present, and future). This kind of reflection mixed with a large portion of imagination can lead to curriculum design that can offer substantial guidance to people on the journey.

This does not necessarily mean that curriculum should grow out of the life of one particular community because persons, whether consciously or unconsciously, are part of larger communities (denominational bodies, cooperating church councils, and the global church). This does not, therefore, rule out denominational or cooperative curriculum designs. What it does suggest is that the curriculum designers need to be in touch with the particular and global forces that influence the persons on the journey. They need, also, to be in touch with the historical tradition and the ways in which it has shaped the present community. They need to image designs that facilitate these persons in understanding and responding to these forces.

If the designers are functioning in a particular context, they need to intentionally study and respond to the forces from larger church bodies and the force acting on these bodies. If, for example, the identity of the denomination is confused and various pressure groups are confusing it further, this will impact the congregation or local parish in many direct and indirect ways. Curriculum designers need, also, to study and respond to the historical events and the events in the contemporary globe that may or may not be directly felt in their particular congregation. Historical-theological disputes or debates about church organization will have left their mark. Wars or hunger or political change in various parts of the globe will affect the particular community, whether or not that community is aware of it. In short, the curriculum designers need to heed John Donne's words.

> No man is an island, entire of itself; every man is a piece of the continent, a part of the main. If a clod be washed away by the sea, Europe is the less, as well as if a promontory were, as well as if a manor of thy friend's or of thine own were; any man's death diminishes me, because I am involved in mankind, and therefore never send to know for whom the bell tolls; it tolls for thee.[19]

If the designers are functioning in a larger community context (e.g., denominational or cooperative), they need to study and respond to the forces acting on particular communities within that larger community. Curriculum designers need to be offered intense experience in many different contexts before they formulate their design. Perhaps they need to be trained in the participant observation methods of anthropology and need to be participant observers in different communities. Certainly, the designers need to represent different communities (geographically, ethnically, socioeconomically, and so forth). Then they can begin to dream together. Although their dreams can never produce a universal blueprint, creative guidance is certainly possible. Any design that emerges should include suggestions for the adaptation of the curriculum design in varying communities. Further, the design should include training and resources that would facilitate persons in reading their own contexts and in adapting and designing in relation to that context.

If a perfect curriculum design existed, someone would have discovered it long ago. We need to stop looking for the magical design that will solve our problems and begin working at the art of designing. The former suggests a static, universal way of looking at curriculum, and the latter suggests a dynamic, flexible mode.

Resources. All this discussion leads us back to that with which most curriculum discussions begin, curriculum resources. What kind of resources, or tools for communication, are needed in a traditioning model of education? The most obvious answer is that the resources need to be historical, contemporary, and visionary. To conceive of curriculum resources without dealing with contemporary issues and future visions is to lock curriculum into continuity without change. To conceive of curriculum resources without dealing with the historical tradition is to lock curriculum into change without continuity. Either option is equally confining. At least three kinds of resources, then, are important for Christian religious education.

First, any resources that facilitate the transmission and interpretation of the historical tradition are important. Certainly this includes stories in all their forms, liturgy, visual arts, dance, and music. Communication of the historical tradition can take place through reading biographies, through telling biblical stories, through describing the origin of the church's creeds, through participating in liturgy, and through experiencing historical art forms and creating contemporary forms that tell the story.

None of this is complete, however, without encouraging persons to consider how they experience these things and how they think others have experienced and will experience them. None of this is complete without imagining what kind of future is pointed to in these historical expressions. This can be done through discussion but also through simulation games (e.g., reenacting the councils of Nicaea and Constantinople as they struggled with what was to become the Nicene Creed), through drama and role play, through the retelling of stories in contemporary settings, through the creation of liturgy and art that take seriously the historical forms, through historical-critical study of the times and people, and so forth. Each of these methods appeals to different senses and uncovers different insights, so no one method or style of resource is adequate. Resources need to be varied and creative at the same time that they facilitate the transmission and interpretation of the historical tradition and help people interpret their own experience and think toward the future.

Secondly, any resources that facilitate the transmission and interpretation of contemporary culture are important. Again these can include any of the varied forms of cultural expression: films, music from various countries or ethnic groups, stories that parents tell their children, media communication (radio and television), conversations with people about the life issues that concern them most, descriptions of the social and physical conditions affecting certain groups of people, and so forth.

Whatever forms these resources may take, persons must be encouraged to engage themselves with the people and the issues by considering how they and others experience these things. Also important is reflection on the relationship between these contemporary cultural expressions and their historical antecedents and between these expressions and the

Christian tradition. For example, consider the event of a national election. What are the issues for you and for others, and how do you respond to these issues? What was the nature of leadership and the election of leaders in biblical times, e.g., the election of Saul as the first king of Israel? What were the issues then? How do they relate to the issues we raise now? What was the nature of leadership and the election of leaders during the Reformation? Compare Luther's Germany and Calvin's Geneva. How do these inform the situation in our country today? What kind of leadership would be ideal in our world? What kind of leadership might help us to the Kingdom of God?

The danger of this kind of contemporary focus is obvious. One need only read through the questions above to find hints of the dangers. People are often deeply invested in these issues and have often carefully separated them from what they see as their religious concerns. People often have divergent opinions and do not want to risk alienating friends. Parents often prefer for their children to learn the Bible at church and to learn other things elsewhere. Using contemporary resources to raise questions of the historical Christian tradition chops away at compartmentalization. This kind of resource is a statement that no part of life (political, artistic, economic, and so forth) is unrelated to the Christian tradition. No part of life, then, is beyond the scope of Christian religious education. The persons who participate in that living faith tradition must deal with all areas of life as they struggle with their own life and with the meaning of being part of the Christian tradition.

In addition to historical and contemporary resources, we need visionary resources that facilitate the dreaming of dreams and the seeing of visions. These are very important to traditioning education and can take many forms. Visionary resources can be studies of biblical and historical visions of the Kingdom of God and the challenge that these visions embody. They can be guided meditations into a fantasy world of future. They can be tools for analyzing a particular contemporary situation and for projecting a desirable future and the actions necessary to move toward that future.

Many more options are available, but in any case, future-oriented resources need to invite reflection, reflection on one's own future vision and that of others. Exploring George Orwell's *1984* or Aldous Huxley's *Brave New World* is interesting, but the significance lies in the engagement with one's own experience that the books stir. Attention needs to be given in our resources to stirring this kind of engagement and at the same time inducing reflection on the Christian tradition and vision. These futuristic resources, then, become the grist for transformation as they pull us into reflection about the future.

Note that in all this discussion of resources a repeated plea is made for the importance of resources that engage persons and their different senses, that stir and inform reflection and visioning, and that facilitate participation in the living tradition. This last theme has to do with helping persons be in touch with the faith community's past and with the immediate experience of themselves and others and open to transforming and being transformed. No matter which of the three kinds of resources (historical, contemporary, or visionary) are being used at a particular time, the resource is most helpful if it somehow engages persons in bringing together past, present, and future in a way that the tradition is reclaimed and transformed.

Conclusions: Characteristics of Traditioning Curriculum

Curriculum in a traditioning model of education will have at least three characteristics. It will relate to the persons at the intersection, facilitate interactions, and promote knowledge with understanding and transformation.

To say that traditioning curriculum will relate to persons at the intersection is to say that it will be designed with those persons in mind. It will be designed appropriate to the developmental levels of the people who will use it, to what is anticipated about their concerns, motivations, abilities, and questions. It will be designed appropriate to the broad cultural context of those people and adaptable to the many particular contexts.

To say that traditioning curriculum will facilitate interactions is to say that it will be designed to help teachers interact with students, to help persons interact within themselves and with others, and to encourage persons to interact with the historical faith tradition, the contemporary world, and the community's hopes for the future. This means that curriculum makers must study and deal with past, present, and future. They must keep in mind those persons who will be part of the curriculum and will use the printed resources. Further, they must recognize that the curriculum will indeed include these people and will enrich their journey as well as be enriched by what these people contribute of themselves to the curriculum.

To say that traditioning curriculum will promote knowledge with understanding and tranformation is to say that it should inform, enrich, and create openings. Curriculum, then, needs to communicate the accumulating wisdom of the Christian faith community and to create openings for persons to understand and enter more fully into the transforming power of the community's tradition.

Notes

Chapter 1

1. James A. Sanders, "Hermeneutics in True and False Prophecy," in *Canon and Authority*, ed. George W. Coats and Burke O. Long (Philadelphia: Fortress Press, 1977), pp. 21-41.
2. Ibid., p. 27.
3. Ibid., p. 29.
4. Friedrich Schleiermacher had profound impact on the methods and concepts of modern theology, particularly with his idea that human experience should be the focus of theological reflection. The question of what is the starting point for theological reflection has been a prominent issue ever since. See particularly *The Christian Faith*, ed. H. R. Mackintosh and J. S. Stewart (New York: Harper & Row, 1963). Schleiermacher believed that the philosophical search for God derives from the feeling of absolute dependence (vol. 1, pp. 16-18) and that one's own deepest experience is united with all reality, including divine reality (vol. 2, pp. 738, 385-86, 569-70). The task of theology for Schleiermacher, then, is to understand experience.
5. George Albert Coe, *What Is Christian Education?* (New York: Charles Scribner's Sons, 1929).
6. Josef R. Geiselmann, *The Meaning of Tradition* (New York: Herder & Herder, 1966), pp. 10-11; Yves M.-J. Congar, *The Meaning of Tradition*, trans. A. N. Woodrow (New York: Hawthorn Books, 1965), pp. 14-16; *The Oxford Dictionary of the Bible*, ed. F.L. Cross and E. A. Livingston (London: Oxford University Press, 1974), pp. 1388-89.
7. Geiselmann, *Meaning of Tradition*, pp. 97-98.
8. Congar, *Meaning of Tradition*, pp. 14-16.
9. Yves M.-J. Congar, *Tradition and Traditions: An Historical and Theological Essay*, trans. Michael Naseby and Thomas Rain-

borough (New York: The Macmillan Co., 1967), p. 241; see also pp. 240, 315.

10. Congar, *Meaning of Tradition,* pp. 17-18.

Chapter 2

1. John Dewey, *Experience and Education* (New York: The Macmillan Co., Collier. Macmillan, [1938], 1963), p. 17.

2. Ibid., pp. 17-23.

3. C. Ellis Nelson, "Our Oldest Problem," in *Tradition and Transformation in Religious Education* (Birmingham, Ala.: Religious Education Press, 1979), p. 58.

4. Ibid., p. 59; C. Ellis Nelson, *Where Faith Begins* (Richmond: John Knox Press, 1968), pp. 67-94. See also Letty Russell's critique of either/or dichotomies, "Handing on Traditions and Changing the World," in O'Hare, pp. 73-86.

5. George Albert Coe, *What Is Christian Education?* (New York: Charles Scribner's Sons, 1929), p. 21.

6. George Albert Coe, *Education in Religion and Morals* (New York: Revell, 1907), pp. 14-17, 21-25, 106-7, 119. The transmission of religious heritage is included in this for Coe, but human development is understood to be more central than instruction. See these emphases also in *A Social Theory of Religious Education* (New York: Charles Scribner's Sons, 1917).

7. Coe, *Education in Religion and Morals,* pp. 124-25.

8. William Clayton Bower, *Character Through Creative Experience* (Chicago: University of Chicago Press, 1930).

9. Horace Bushnell, *Christian Nurture* (New York: Charles Scribner's Sons, 1903), p. 10.

10. Harrison S. Elliott, *Can Religious Education Be Christian?* (New York: The Macmillan Co., 1940), pp. 40-51.

11. Robert W. Lynn and Elliott Wright, *The Big Little School: Two Hundred Years of the Sunday School,* 2d ed. rev. and enl. (Nashville: Abingdon; Birmingham, Ala.: Religious Education Press, 1980), pp. 70-76.

12. Ibid., pp. 90-108.

13. Gerald E. Knoff, *The World Sunday School Movement* (New York: The Seabury Press, 1979), pp. 23-24, 60.

14. Boardman W. Kathan, "The Sunday School Revisited," *Religious Education* 75:1 (January–February 1980): 13. Jack Seymour argues that the concern for human experience is not as lacking in the nineteenth- and twentieth-century Sunday school

movement as is often thought. See *From Sunday School to Church School: Continuities in Protestant Church Education, 1860–1929* (Washington, D.C., University Press of America, 1982).

15. Lynn and Wright, *The Big Little School,* pp. 70-76, 120-29.

16. Johannes Hofinger, *The Art of Teaching Christian Doctrine: The Good News and Its Proclamation* (Notre Dame, Ind.: University of Notre Dame Press, 1957), p. 8; see also *Our Message Is Christ* (Notre Dame, Ind.: Fides Publishers, 1974), pp. 6-11; Josef A. Jungmann, *Announcing the Word of God* (New York: Herder & Herder, 1967), pp. 59-65; and *Handing on the Faith* (New York: Herder & Herder, 1959).

17. Hofinger, *Art of Teaching Doctrine,* pp. 1-48.

18. H. Shelton Smith, *Faith and Nurture* (New York: Charles Scribner's Sons, 1941), pp. 64-65.

19. See particularly John Frederick Herbart, *Outline of Educational Doctrine* (New York: The Macmillan Co., 1901); Harold B. Dunkel, *Herbart and Education* (New York: Random House, 1969); and Robert Ulich, *History of Educational Thought* (New York: American Book Co., 1950), pp. 272-82.

20. Kendig Brubaker Cully, *The Search for a Christian Education— Since 1940* (Philadelphia: The Westminster Press, 1965), pp. 102, 158-59.

21. Paul H. Vieth, ed., *The Church and Christian Education* (St. Louis: Bethany Press, 1947), p. 52. Since this book is a committee report, Vieth presents different viewpoints on the various issues. The differences often reflect some of the same tensions that are dealt with in this chapter.

22. Elliott, *Can Religious Education Be Christian?* pp. 225-26, 229-32.

23. Ibid., pp. 213, 229-32, 251-58.

24. Ibid., pp. 205-11.

25. Ibid., p. 205.

26. Smith, *Faith and Nurture,* pp. 60, 114-35.

27. Ibid., p. 46.

28. Ibid., pp. 114, 79.

29. Ibid., pp. 146-51.

30. Ibid., pp. 181-82.

31. Dewey, *Experience and Education,* pp. 25-31, 89-90.

32. Ibid., pp. 27-28, 49-50.

33. Ibid., p. 35.

34. Ibid., pp. 42, 45.

35. Ibid., p. 82, 73-75.
36. Ibid., pp.58-60.
37. Thomas H. Groome, "Christian Education: A Task of Present Dialectical Hermeneutics," *Living Light* 14:3 (Fall 1977): 412.
38. Ibid.
39. John H. Westerhoff, *Will Our Children Have Faith?* (New York: The Seabury Press, 1976), p. 51. This quote was taken from Nelson, *Where Faith Begins,* p. 10.
40. Westerhoff, *Will Our Children Have Faith?* p. 51.
41. See particularly John H. Westerhoff and Gwen K. Neville, *Generation to Generation* (Philadelphia: United Church Press, 1974); and Gwen K. Neville and John H. Westerhoff, *Learning Through Liturgy* (New York: The Seabury Press, 1978).
42. Nelson, *Where Faith Begins,* p. 69.
43. Ibid., p. 79.
44. Nelson, in O'Hare, p. 60.
45. Nelson, *Where Faith Begins,* p. 94.
46. Ibid., p. 87.
47. Nelson, in O'Hare, pp. 61, 65.
48. Thomas H. Groome, "The Critical Principle in Christian Education and the Task of Prophecy," *Religious Education* 72:3 (May–June 1977): 262-66.
49. Ibid., pp. 266-68. This model is developed extensively in *Christian Religious Education* (San Francisco: Harper & Row, 1980). The emphasis on dialogue and on the unity of action and reflection is shared with Paulo Freire, *Pedagogy of the Oppressed* (New York: Herder & Herder, 1970), pp. 75-76.
50. Mary C. Boys, "Access to Traditions and Transformation," in O'Hare, pp. 9-34.
51. Philip Phenix, "Transcendence and the Curriculum," in *Curriculum Theorizing,* ed. William Pinar (Berkeley: McCutchan, 1975), pp. 323-24.
52. Dwayne Huebner, "Curriculum as Concern for Man's Temporality," in Pinar, p. 249.
53. Bernard E. Meland, *Higher Education and the Human Spirit* (Chicago: University of Chicago Press, 1953), p. 51.
54. Ibid., pp. 79-109.
55. Maria Harris, "Word, Sacrament, Prophecy," in O'Hare, pp. 35-57.
56. Russell, in O'Hare, p. 73.
57. Dwayne Huebner, "The Language of Religious Eduation," in O'Hare, pp. 98-99.

58. Ibid., pp. 88-96, 109-11.
59. Nelson, in O'Hare p. 65.
60. Boys, in O'Hare, p. 27.

Chapter 3

1. Macquarrie has built his understanding of the Christian community and the theological task of that community on this concept of *laos*. The people of God provide the starting point of theological reflection. See John Macquarrie, *The Faith of the People of God* (New York: Charles Scribner's Sons, 1972), pp. 16-23.
2. Avery Dulles, *Models of the Church* (Garden City, N.Y.: Doubleday & Co., 1974), p. 8.
3. Paul Minear, *Images of the Church in the New Testament* (Philadelphia: The Westminster Press, 1960), pp. 221-22.
4. Ibid., pp. 222-23.
5. Dulles, *Models of the Church,* p. 15.
6. Congar, *Tradition and Traditions,* pp. 251-52.
7. Jürgen Moltmann, *Theology of Hope* (New York: Harper & Row, 1967), pp. 30, 89.
8. John Macquarrie, *Principles of Christian Theology* (New York: Charles Scribner's Sons, 1977), p. 1.
9. Maurice Wiles, *What Is Theology?* (London: Oxford University Press, 1976), p. 9.
10. John B. Cobb, Jr., professor of theology, in a class lecture at the School of Theology at Claremont, September 1975. Kaufman also recognizes that theology is formed from inside faith. He distinguishes between theology and the scientific study of religion that is performed from outside faith. Gordon Kaufman, *God the Problem* (Cambridge: Harvard University Press, 1972), pp. 17-37. Similarly, Macquarrie distinguishes between theology and the philosophy of religion that demands more detachment. Macquarrie, *Principles of Christian Theology,* p. 2.
11. Wiles, *What Is Theology?* p. 7.
12. Ibid., p. 9.
13. Macquarrie, *Principles of Christian Theology,* pp. 12-13.
14. James Fowler has particularly expounded this point of view. He describes faith as a verb rather than a noun. He defines it as "an active 'mode of being in relation' to another or others in which we invest commitment, belief, love, risk and hope"; James W. Fowler and Sam Keen, *Life Maps* (Waco, Tex.: Word Books,

1978), p. 18. See also James W. Fowler, *Stages of Faith* (San Francisco: Harper & Row, 1981), pp. 16-17. This point of view is quite compatible with the active view of faith in Macquarrie, who talks about faith in terms of commitment, ultimate concern, belief, and response (see *Principles of Christian Theology,* pp. 28-29). Likewise, Tillich's equation of faith with ultimate concern and Pannenberg's equation of faith with trust are dynamic views that incorporate all dimensions of human response to life. See Paul Tillich, *Dynamics of Faith* (New York: Harper & Row, 1957), pp. 1-20; and Wolfhart Pannenberg, *The Apostles' Creed* (Philadelphia: The Westminster Press, 1972), pp. 3-7.

15. Furthermore, this dichotomy represents only one set of methodological issues in theology, and even this issue has more dimensions than will be dealt with here. An example of another, related methodological issue is the way in which theological method is influenced by philosophy. This issue is treated extensively in John B. Cobb, Jr., *Living Options in Protestant Theology* (Philadelphia: The Westminster Press, 1962). Cobb's highlighting of this issue leads into some differences in groupings and emphases.

16. See particularly Karl Barth, *The Doctrine of Reconciliation of the Word of God* (Edinburgh: Clark, 1936), pp. 98-140, 284-315; Emil Brunner, *The Christian Doctrine of the Church, Faith, and the Consummation* (Philadelphia: The Westminster Press, 1950), pp. 43-59. Both Barth and Brunner favored a critical approach to Scripture and one that acknowledges the relation of the scriptural witness to the historical church tradition and God's ongoing revelation through the Holy Spirit. The weight of their work, however, is to emphasize the normative nature of God's revelation in Christ as witnessed to in Scripture.

17. The significance of doctrine as a guide is particularly reflected in the decrees of Vatican I and the theologizing that followed. Here the emphasis was on the permanence of the meaning in the church's dogmas, suggesting their timeless relevance for the life of the Christian community. For an exposition of this idea of permanence of dogma see Bernard J. F. Lonergan, *Method of Theology* (London: Darton, Longman, & Todd, 1972), pp. 302-3.

The importance of doctrine for the practice of the church was emphasized in a new way by Jungmann, Hofinger, and others in the kerygmatic renewal. They reacted against teaching doctrine in all its complexity but maintained an essentially doctrinal approach. Hofinger sought the kerygma, or the central Christian message, in the Bible and church doctrine as the guide for Christian life and the focus of Christian religious education. He was not separating doctrine from the Bible, but he did find in the church's doctrine the basic elements of the Christian message to be passed on in catechetics. See particularly Johannes Hofinger, *Our Message Is Christ;* and *The Art of Teaching Christian Doctrine.*

18. Macquarrie, *Principles of Christian Theology,* pp. 11-12.

19. Kaufman, *God the Problem,* pp. 20-24.

20. Schleiermacher, *The Christian Faith,* vol. 1, pp. 16-18.

21. Ibid., vol. 2, p. 738; see also pp. 385-86 and 569-70.

22. This does not mean for Schleiermacher that the Word revealed in Jesus Christ should be ignored in theological reflection. It simply means that human experience or the religious affections provide an adequate starting point for this reflection. (See particularly ibid., vol. 1, pp. 76-78, 127-28, 131-41.) This is possible because all existence is a reflection of God. All of creation reflects the Word. (See ibid., vol. 1, pp. 149-56.)

23. Don S. Browning, "Analogy, Symbol, and Pastoral Theology in Tillich's Thought," *Pastoral Psychology* 19:181 (February 1968): 41-54.

24. Kaufman, *God the Problem,* pp. 25-26.

25. Schubert Ogden, "What is Theology?" *Journal of Religion* 52 (1972): 22-40.

26. See particularly Daniel Day Williams, *The Minister and the Care of Souls* (New York: Harper & Row, 1961); Anton Boisen, *The Exploration of the Inner World* (New York: Harper & Brothers, 1936).

27. Allen Moore, "The Sociological Context of Theology" (Lecture delivered at the Conference on Sociology of Theology, Urban Theology Unit, Sheffield, England, March 1975); Don Browning, *The Moral Context of Pastoral Care* (Philadelphia: The Westminster Press, 1976).

28. Snyder has spoken of this idea in many of his writings and lectures but develops the idea particularly in "Educating a People of God," mimeographed (Chicago: Chicago Theological Seminary, 1962).

29. Ross Snyder, "A Ministry of Meanings," mimeographed (Nashville: Youth Department, Division of the Local Church, General Board of Education of The Methodist Church, 1961).

30. Ross Snyder, "The Authentic Life: Its Theory and Practice," mimeographed (Nashville: Older Youth–Young Adult Project, General Board of Education of The Methodist Church, 1963).

31. Cobb has made this point with particular clarity: "Most serious thinkers are concerned about the relations of a variety of authorities rather than simply the selection of one. A position would not be Christian at all if it did not accept some authority of at least some aspect of the Bible. At the same time it would not be theological at all if it consisted entirely of Biblical texts unselectively assembled. Any serious statement of Christian theology must have some concern for the present cultural-intellectual-spiritual situation of man as well as some concern for the Bible" (*Living Options,* p. 11).

32. Paul J. Achtemeier, *An Introduction to the New Hermeneutic* (Philadelphia: The Westminster Press, 1969), pp. 13-14.

33. James Sanders, "Hermeneutics," in *Interpreter's Dictionary of the Bible Supplementary Volume,* ed. Keith Crim (Nashville: Abingdon, 1976), p. 402.

34. See particularly Nelson, *Where Faith Begins*; and Edward Everding, "A Hermeneutical Approach to Educational Theory," in *Foundations for Christian Education in an Era of Change,* ed. Marvin J. Taylor (Nashville: Abingdon, 1976), pp. 41-53.

35. Carl Braaten has recognized the tendency for the scope of hermeneutics to be enlarged to include history and historical documents; see *History and Hermeneutics* (Philadelphia: The Westminster Press, 1966), p. 131. Palmer notes that the word *hermeneutics* has come to refer to the interpretation of a broad variety of texts, particularly literary texts, but also including human art, action, dreams, and symbols. See particularly his review of six modern definitions of hermeneutics in Richard Palmer, *Hermeneutics* (Evanston, Ill.: Northwestern University Press, 1969), pp. 33-45.

A new trend is emerging in which the present action of the Christian community and the action upon that community are interpreted as texts. Pastoral theologians have often referred to their pastoral experiences with persons as texts to be interpreted. Charles Caldwell argues for an interpretation of both the case and the tradition, and he sees the Word of God at the interface; see *Pastoral Theological Hermeneutics* (Ann Arbor: University Microfilms International, 1978), p. 129. Similar to Caldwell's pastoral theological hermeneutics in Thomas Groome's present dialectical hermeneutics that is influenced by the liberation theologians' understanding of praxis. Groome, like Caldwell, is concerned with the interpretation of both the present experience of the Christian community and the texts of tradition. He, however, describes the contemporary texts not so much in terms of pastoral cases as in terms of the actions of the Christian community and the actions of the culture on that community. He also stresses the proclamation and interpretation of future hope so that he attempts to bring together past, present, and future as texts to be interpreted and related to one another. See particularly Groome's article in *Living Light*, pp. 416-21; and *Christian Education: A Task of Present Dialectical Hermeneutics*, pp. 195-97, 217-23.

36. Sanders, in *IDBS*, p. 404; see also Sanders, in Coats and Long, pp. 21-41; and "Adaptable for Life: The Nature and Function of Canon," in *Magnalia Dei*, ed. F. M. Cross, W. E. Lemke, and P. D. Miller (Garden City, N.Y.: Doubleday & Co., 1976), pp. 531-60.

37. Sanders, in *IDBS*, p. 403.

38. The idea of acting in the direction of the Kingdom of God is emphasized by Moltmann. He understands God's covenant with humanity as calling human persons to move in the direction of God's promise (*Theology of Hope*, pp. 100-121).

39. For Jose Miguez-Bonino and Gustavo Gutiérrez this means that God is actually present in history, transforming the world, and that human persons are called to participate in that work for transformation. See particularly Jose Miguez-Bonino, *Doing Theology in a Revolutionary Situation* (Philadelphia: Fortress Press, 1975), pp. 89, 150, 108-9; and Gustavo Gutiérrez, *A Theology of Liberation* (Maryknoll, N.Y.: Orbis Books, 1973), pp. 189-208. For Moltmann, God is understood as future but revealed in the event of promise and in relation to the human experience of the world at a given time (*Theology of Hope*, p. 89; see also pp. 95-138). This event of promise does not separate people from the world but involves them in hope, mission, and self-emptying (pp. 91-92).

40. Gutiérrez, *Theology of Liberation*, p. 160; Moltmann, *Theology of Hope*, pp. 92-94, 102-12.

41. Moltmann, *Theology of Hope*, p. 100.

42. Ibid., p. 147.

43. Ibid., pp. 37-41. Moltmann puts this idea over against an idea of

Logos as "the epiphany of the eternal present of being" (pp. 40-41).

44. Gutiérrez, *Theology of Liberation,* p. 91.
45. Ibid., pp. 161, 168, 177, 226-32, 38.
46. Ibid., p. 238.
47. Groome, *Christian Religious Education,* p. 45. Groome sees his position as in line with that of the Second Vatican Council as stated in *Constitution on the Church in the Modern World* (arts. 38 and 39). He particularly refers to the ideas in that document that human efforts will bear fruit and prepare the "material" for the Kingdom.

Chapter 4

1. Dwayne Huebner, in Pinar, p. 241.
2. Paul Filmer et al., *New Directions in Sociological Theory* (Cambridge: MIT Press, 1973), p. 2.
3. Klaus F. Riegel, "Toward a Dialectical Theory of Development," *Human Development* 18 (1975): 50.
4. Ibid., pp. 50-64. See also "The Dialectics of Human Development," *American Psychologist* 31:10 (October 1976).
5. Riegel, in *Human Development,* pp. 51-52; see also "From Traits and Equilibrium Toward Developmental Dialectics," in *1974-75 Nebraska Symposium on Motivation,* ed. W. J. Arnold and J. K. Cole (Lincoln: University of Nebraska Press, 1976); and *Psychology of Development and History* (New York: Plenum, 1976).
6. Donald T. Campbell, "On the Conflicts Between Biological and Social Evolution and Between Psychology and Moral Tradition," *American Psychologist* 30 (December 1975): 1103-26, esp. pp. 1120-22.
7. Ibid., p. 1120.
8. Robert Jay Lifton, "Protean Man," *Partisan Review* 35:1 (Winter 1968): 13-27.
9. Ibid., p. 19.
10. Ibid., p. 16.
11. Ibid.
12. Klaus F. Riegel, "Developmental Psychology and Society: Some Historical and Ethical Considerations," in *Life Span Developmental Psychology,* ed. J. R. Nesselroade and H. W. Reese (New York: Academic Press, 1973), pp. 20-23.

13. Eugene Fontinell, "Pragmatism, Process, and Religious Education," *Religious Education* 68:3 (May–June 1973): 324.
14. Ibid.
15. Riegel, in Nesselroade and Reese, pp. 14-15, 22-23. The mind-body problem is reformed in Rubinstein's perspective. Mind and body are not seen as two separate entities. The mutual influence of consciousness and behavior is so great that the line between the mental and the physical is not clearly discernible. Both are in relationship to both inner and outer dimensions of reality, and the dualism is between the inner and outer rather than between the mind and body.
16. Leonard Broom and Philip Selznick, *Sociology* (New York: Harper & Row, 1977), p. 100.
17. George H. Mead, "Scientific Method and Individual Thinker," in *Creative Intelligence,* ed. John Dewey et al. (New York: Holt, Rinehart and Winston, 1917), p. 176.
18. Ibid., p. 225.
19. George H. Mead, *The Philosophy of the Act* (Chicago: University of Chicago Press, 1938), pp. 64-65.
20. Ibid., p. 638.
21. George H. Mead, *The Social Psychology of George Herbert Mead* (Chicago: University of Chicago Press, 1956), p. 21.
22. George H. Mead, *The Philosophy of the Present* (LaSalle, Ill.: Open Court Publishing Co., 1932), pp. 1-2.
23. Ibid., p.23.
24. George H. Mead, *Mind, Self, and Society* (Chicago: University of Chicago Press, 1934), p. 73; cf. p. 49; and *Social Psychology,* pp. 32, 217, 255-56.
25. Arnold M. Rose, ed. "A Systematic Summary of Symbolic Interaction Theory," in *Human Behavior and Social Processes* (London: Routledge & Kegan Paul, 1962), p. 13.
26. Mead, *Mind, Self, and Society,* p. 6.
27. Mead, *Social Psychology,* pp. 37-38.
28. Ibid., pp. 241-42.
29. Mead, *Philosophy of the Present,* p. xxv.
30. Mead, *Social Psychology,* pp. 32-33, 37-38.
31. Ibid., p. 34.
32. Mead, *Philosophy of the Act,* p. 616.
33. Mead, *Social Psychology,* p. 33.
34. This idea is developed in Douglas C. Kimmel, *Adulthood and Aging* (New York: John Wiley & Sons, 1974), p. 51.
35. Mead, *Social Psychology,* pp. 224-25, 237-41; "Social Con-

sciousness and the Consciousness of Meaning," *Psychological Bulletin* 7:12 (1910): 397-405.

36. Mead, in *Psychological Bulletin,* p. 399; cf. *Philosophy of the Present,* p. 4.
37. Mead, in *Psychological Bulletin,* p. 403.
38. Ibid., p. 405.
39. Mead sees this as the process of hypothesis-testing, which is the way persons seek to universalize their thoughts without absolutizing them (in Dewey et al., pp. 214-15).
40. This idea of communicating meanings and values through symbols is a basic assumption of symbolic interaction theory. See Rose, p. 8.
41. Mead, *Philosophy of the Act,* p. 124. Mead understands the social act to include the influences of the past on a person's perception, habitual stimulus-response patterns, and the active mental process of interpreting and reconstructing interaction patterns (ibid., pp. 3-4).
42. Mead, *Philosophy of the Present,* p. 49; cf. pp. 51, 64-65.
43. Ibid., p. 90.
44. Kimmel, *Adulthood and Aging,* p. 58.
45. This is what Whitehead means when he says that the world is "divisible but not divided." Alfred North Whitehead, *Process and Reality* (New York: The Macmillan Co., 1929), p. 96.
46. Ibid., p. 365; cf. *Religion in the Making* (New York: The Macmillan Co., 1926), p. 109; *Adventures of Ideas* (New York: The Free Press, 1933), pp. 192-93.
47. Whitehead, *Process and Reality,* p. 32.
48. Whitehead argues that a factual interpretation of reality requires that the interpreter deal with these contrasting qualities (ibid., pp. 513-15).
49. Ibid., p. 515.
50. Ibid., p. 318.
51. Ibid., p. 127.
52. Ibid., pp. 33-34, 92.
53. Ibid., p. 207.
54. Ibid., p. 321.
55. Ibid., pp. 134, 37.
56. For Whitehead the occasion itself has a threefold character: (a) the given past, (b) the subjective character aimed at concrescence, and (c) the superjective character that is its pragmatic contribution to creativity (ibid., p. 134; cf. pp. 248-52).
57. Ibid., pp. 31-32, 135, 143.

58. Ibid., p. 165; cf. Whitehead, *Adventures of Ideas,* pp. 192-94.

59. Whitehead, *Process and Reality,* p. 164.

60. John B. Cobb, Jr., and David R. Griffin, *Process Theology* (Philadelphia: The Westminster Press, 1976), pp. 28-29.

61. Whitehead describes this process as canalization (*Process and Reality,* pp. 163-64).

62. Human beings are understood as complexes of many enduring objects. Whitehead defines an enduring object as "a linear succession of actual occasions forming a historical route in which some defining characteristic is inherited by each occasion from its predecessors" (ibid., p. 301). A complex of enduring objects is called a corpuscular society (pp. 166-67, 301).

63. Ibid., p. 285.

64. A person is a living society of both organic and inorganic occasions. In the organic occasions, reversion takes place in the mental pole so that novelty is introduced. An organism is alive where novelty arises within it that cannot be explained simply by its past or physical inheritance (ibid., pp. 153-57, 159).

65. Whitehead describes the enduring personality as "the historic route of living occasions which are severally dominant in the body at successive instants" (ibid., p. 182; see also pp. 166-67). The human person is a complex social organization in which the elements of continuity and change are coordinated through this enduring personality.

66. In Whitehead's words, contrasts are "modes of synthesis of entities in one prehension" (ibid., p. 33).

67. Ibid., p. 167; cf. pp. 163-76.

68. Ibid., p. 309; cf. Cobb and Griffin, *Process Theology,* p. 23.

69. Whitehead, *Adventures of Ideas,* pp. 191-95.

70. Norman Pittenger, *The Christian Church as Social Process* (Philadelphia: The Westminster Press, 1971), pp. 78-79.

71. Charles Hartshorne, *Creative Synthesis and Philosophic Method* (LaSalle, Ill.: Open Court Publishing Co., 1970), p. 318.

72. Whitehead, *Religion in the Making,* p. 140.

73. This is the purpose of education according to Whitehead in *The Aims of Education* (New York: The Macmillan Co., 1929). p. v.

Chapter 5

1. Westerhoff, *Will Our Children Have Faith?* pp. 6-25.

2. This idea has been developed particularly by Ross Snyder. See, for example *Young People and Their Culture* (Nashville:

Abingdon Press, 1969), pp. 162-63. In an earlier unpublished book, Snyder talks about "ministry of the pulse of tradition." This ministry involves helping people discover and enter into the pulse of tradition, which is an active world of persons, meanings, and intention. This involvement in the pulse of tradition enriches both the persons and the tradition. See "Educating a People of God" (Chicago: Chicago Theological Seminary, 1962) (Mimeographed).

3. Snyder, *Young People and Their Culture*, p. 69. Snyder develops the idea of story in his writings of the 1960s, but in the 70s he shifts his language from *stories* to *sagas*. He understands a person's saga to be his or her life story, with particular focus on the meanings in that story and on that person's relatedness to self, others, and God.

4. Dewey emphasized this in his philosophy of education. See particularly *Experience and Education*.

5. Meland, *Higher Education and the Human Spirit*, pp. 79-109.

6. See particularly Ross Snyder, "Boisen's Understanding of Religious Experience," *Chicago Theological Seminary Register* 67:1 (1977): 33-51.

7. Thomas H. Groome, *Christian Religious Education;* cf. Groome's article in *Living Light*, pp. 408-23.

8. See, for example, Theodore Brameld, *Toward a Reconstructed Philosophy of Education* (New York: Dryden Press, 1956).

9. Moltmann, *Theology of Hope*, pp. 330-31.

10. Ibid., pp. 120-21.

11. Westerhoff, *Will Our Children Have Faith?* p. 80.

12. Groome, *Christian Religious Education*.

13. Huebner, in Pinar, pp. 237-49.

14. Paul Irwin, *The Care and Counseling of Youth in the Church* (Philadelphia: Fortress Press, 1975). Irwin advocates a nurturing ministry to the whole person that he calls personal ministry (p. xiii); Martin A. Lang, "Faith as a Learned Life-Style," in *Emerging Issues in Religious Education*, ed. Gloria Durka and Joanmarie Smith (Paramus, N.J.: Paulist/Newman Press, 1976), pp. 69-75. Lang understands the most basic functional level of religious education to be faith-sharing, which is personal, one-to-one communication.

15. Snyder, *Young People and Their Culture*, p. 53.

16. Whitehead, *Aims of Education*, pp. 15-28.

17. Jerome Bruner, *Toward a Theory of Instruction* (New York: W. W. Norton & Co., 1969), pp. 39-72.

18. James Michael Lee, *The Flow of Religious Instruction* (Dayton: Pflaum Press, 1973), pp. 39-57. Lee wants theories of teaching to be considered because they offer guidance as to how teachers can facilitate the learning process in others (p.48).
19. Lewis Sherrill, *The Rise of Christian Education* (New York: The Macmillan Co., 1953), pp. 61-64.
20. Ibid., p. 6.
21. Ibid., pp. 14-16.
22. Ibid., pp. 17-24.
23. Ibid., p. 6.
24. Ibid., pp. 6-7.
25. Alfred N. Whitehead, *Process and Reality,* rev. ed. (New York: The Free Press, 1978), p. 259.
26. Ibid.
27. Winston Churchill, "Examinations and Education at Bangalore," in *Aims of Education,* ed. Leslie M. Brown (New York: Teachers College Press, 1970), p. 128.
28. Philip Phenix, in Pinar, pp. 328-33.
29. Ibid., p. 328.
30. Ibid.

Chapter 6

1. Dwayne Huebner has been a particularly vocal spokesperson for this point of view. See Huebner, in Pinar, p. 244.
2. John Dewey, *Democracy and Education* (New York: The Macmillan Co., 1926 [1916]), p. 127; R. S. Peters, *Ethics and Education* (Glenview, Ill.: Scott, Foresman and Co., 1967 [1966]), p. 5.
3. Walter N. Vernon, "Curriculum Resources, Christian Nurture, and Changing Times," *Perkins Journal* 32:1 (Fall 1978): 8. This trend is evidenced within many Protestant denominations in the United States and Canada, e.g., the loaves-and-fishes curriculum program of the United Church of Canada (produced by the Division of Mission in Canada).
4. Leslie M. Brown, ed., *Aims of Education* (New York: Teachers College Press, 1970), pp. ix-xix. Brown uses a similar delineation of these four concepts, but he speaks of ideals rather than visions. Also, he understands goals to be distinctive by being private rather than public. See particularly p. xvii. The delineation here is not meant to be perfectly consistent with Brown's, but marked similarities do exist. Similarities also exist

with Rubin Gotesky's view put forth in that same volume. See particularly "Means, Ends-in-View, Anticipations and Outcomes," pp. 170-73.

5. Freire, *Pedagogy of the Oppressed*, pp. 58-59.
6. Westerhoff, *Will Our Children Have Faith?* pp. 22-23.
7. Lewis Sherrill, *The Gift of Power* (New York: The Macmillan Co., 1955), pp. 188-89.
8. Westerhoff, *Will Our Children Have Faith?* pp. 51-52.
9. Malcolm L. Warford, *The Necessary Illusion* (Philadelphia: Pilgrim Press, 1976), pp. 53-61.
10. Ibid., p. 61.
11. Freire, *Pedagogy of the Oppressed*, pp. 84-85.

Chapter 7

1. Maxine Greene, "Curriculum and Consciousness," in Pinar, p. 307.
2. Ibid., p. 308.
3. Ibid., p. 311.
4. Ibid., pp. 313-14; See also "Cognition, Consciousness, and Curriculum," in *Heightened Consciousness, Cultural Revolution, and Curriculum Theory*, ed. William Pinar (Berkeley: McCutchan, 1974), pp. 69-84.
5. William Pinar, "Currere: Toward Reconceptualization," in his *Curriculum Theorizing*, pp. 398-99.
6. Ibid., p. 412.
7. Ibid.
8. David Zisenwine identifies deterministic, centralized curriculum as a dominant problem in Jewish curriculum. He thinks this problem has given rise to experimentation and that new models are needed. See "Jewish Education—An Opportunity Model," *Religious Education* 75:5 (September–October 1980): 553-60.

   Mary Jo Osterman identifies the present period in Protestant curriculum development as "Babel II," which is characterized by movement away from centralized planning toward selectivity and grass-roots curriculum. See "The Two Hundred Year Struggle for Protestant Religious Education Curriculum Theory," *Religious Education* 75:5 (September–October 1980): 530, 530n, 537.
9. Barry W. Holtz, "Towards an Integrated Curriculum for the Jewish School," *Religious Education* 75:5 (September–October 1980): 546-47.

10. Ibid., pp. 549-50.
11. See particularly Mary Boys, "Curriculum Thinking from a Roman Catholic Perspective," *Religious Education* 75:5 (September–October 1980): 522-23; William L. Roberts, "From Curriculum Research to Foundational Theorizing," *Religious Education* 75:5 (September–October 1980): 514-15; and Zisenwine, in *Religious Education*, p. 559.
12. Boys, pp. 518, 519, 523-24, 527.
13. The image of wise companion is suggested by both Pinar, p. 412, and Herbert Kliebard, "Metaphorical Roots of Curriculum Design," in Pinar, p. 85.
14. Kliebard, in Pinar, p. 85.
15. Lawrence A. Cremin, "Curriculum Making in the United States," in Pinar, pp. 30-31.
16. Ibid., p. 28.
17. Ibid., pp. 30-31.
18. Ibid., p. 30.
19. John Donne, *Devotions upon Emergent Occasions* (Ann Arbor: University of Michigan Press, 1959), pp. 108-9.

Bibliography

Achtemeier, Paul J. *An Introduction to the New Hermeneutic.* Philadelphia: The Westminster Press, 1969.

Alves, Rubem. *A Theology of Human Hope.* St. Meinrad, Ind.: Abbey Press, 1975.

Barth, Karl. *The Doctrine of the Word of God,* Trans. G. T. Thomson. (Church Dogmatics I/1) Edinburgh: Clark, 1936.

———. *The Doctrine of Reconciliation.* Trans. G. V. Bromiley. (Church Dogmatics IV/3) 2 vols. Edinburgh: Clark, 1962.

Bellah, Robert N. *Beyond Belief.* New York: Harper & Row, 1970.

Boisen, Anton. *The Exploration of the Inner World.* New York: Harper & Brothers, 1936.

Bower, William Clayton. *Character Through Creative Experience.* Chicago: University of Chicago Press, 1930.

Boys, Mary C. "Access to Traditions and Transformation." In *Tradition and Transformation in Religious Education,* ed. Padraic O'Hare. Birmingham, Ala.: Religious Education Press, 1979.

———. "Curriculum Thinking from a Roman Catholic Perspective." *Religious Education* 75:5 (September–October 1980): 516-27.

Braaten, Carl. *History and Hermeneutics.* Philadelphia: The Westminster Press, 1966.

Brameld, Theodore. *Toward a Reconstructed Philosophy of Education.* New York: Dryden Press, 1956.

Broom, Leonard, and Selznick, Philip. *Sociology: A Text with Adapted Readings.* New York: Harper & Row, 1977.

Brown, Leslie M., ed. *Aims of Education.* New York: Teachers College Press, 1970.

Browning, Don S. "Analogy, Symbol, and Pastoral Theology in Tillich's Thought." *Pastoral Psychology,* 19:181 (February 1968): 41-54.

————. *The Moral Context of Pastoral Care.* Philadelphia: The Westminster Press, 1976.

Bruner, Jerome. *Toward a Theory of Instruction.* New York: W. W. Norton & Co., 1969.

Brunner, Emil. *The Christian Doctrine of God.* Trans. Olive Wyon. (Dogmatics I) Philadelphia: The Westminster Press, 1950.

————. *The Christian Doctrine of the Church, Faith, and the Consummation.* Trans. David Cairns and T. H. L. Parker. (Dogmatics III) Philadelphia: The Westminster Press, 1960.

Bultmann, Rudolf. *The Presence of Eternity: History and Eschatology.* New York: Harper & Brothers, 1957.

Bushnell, Horace. *Christian Nurture.* New York: Charles Scribner's Sons, 1903 (1888).

Caldwell, Charles. *Pastoral Theological Hermeneutics: A Quest for Method.* Ann Arbor: University Microfilms International, 1978.

Campbell, Donald T. "On the Conflicts Between Biological and Social Evolution and Between Psychology and Moral Tradition." *American Psychologist* 30:12 (December 1975): 1103-26.

Churchill, Winston. "Examinations and Education at Bangalore." In *Aims of Education,* ed. Leslie M. Brown. New York: Teachers College Press, 1970.

Cobb, John B., Jr., *Living Options in Protestant Theology.* Philadelphia: The Westminster Press, 1962.

Cobb, John B., Jr. and Griffin, David R. *Process Theology: An Introductory Exposition.* Philadelphia: The Westminster Press, 1976.

Coe, George Albert. *Education in Religion and Morals.* Old Tappan, N.J.: Fleming H. Revell, 1907 (1904).

————. *A Social Theory of Religious Education.* New York: Charles Scribner's Sons, 1917.

————. *What Is Christian Education?* New York: Charles Scribner's Sons, 1929.

Congar, Yves M.-J. *The Meaning of Tradition.* Trans. A. N. Woodrow. New York: Hawthorn Books, 1964.

————. *Tradition and Traditions.* New York: The Macmillan Co., 1966.

Cremin, Lawrence A. "Curriculum Making in the United States." In *Curriculum Theorizing,* ed. William Pinar. Berkeley: McCutchan, 1975.

Cross, F. L., and Livingston, E. A. *The Oxford Dictionary of the Bible.* London: Oxford University Press, 1974.

Cully, Kendig Brubaker. *The Search for a Christian Education—Since 1940.* Philadelphia: The Westminster Press, 1965.

Dewey, John. *Democracy and Education.* New York: The Macmillan Co., 1926 (1916).

———. *Experience and Education.* New York: The Macmillan Co., Collier. Macmillan, 1963 (1938).

Donne, John. *Devotions upon Emergent Occasions.* Ann Arbor: University of Michigan Press, 1959.

Dulles, Avery. *Models of the Church.* Garden City, N.J.: Doubleday & Co., 1974.

Dunkel, Harold B. *Herbart and Education.* New York: Random House, 1969.

Ebeling, Bernard. *Introduction to a Theological Theory of Language.* London: Collins, 1973.

Ebeling, Gerhard. *Word and Faith.* Trans. James W. Leitch. Philadelphia: Fortress Press, 1963.

Elliott, Harrison. *Can Religious Education Be Christian?* New York: The Macmillan Co., 1940.

Evans, Robert A., and Parker, Thomas D., eds. *Christian Theology: A Case Study Approach.* New York: Harper & Row, 1976.

Everding, H. Edward, Jr. "A Hermeneutical Approach to Educational Theory." In *Foundations for Christian Education in an Era of Change,* ed. Marvin Taylor. Nashville: Abingdon, 1976.

Fackre, Gabriel, and Chartier, Jan. *Youth Ministry: The Gospel and the People.* Valley Forge, Pa.: Judson Press, 1979.

Farley, Edward. *Requiem for a Lost Piety.* Philadelphia: The Westminster Press, 1966.

Filmer, Paul; Phillipson, Michael; Silverman, David; and Walsh, David, eds. *New Directions in Sociological Theory.* Cambridge: MIT Press, 1973.

Fontinell, Eugene. "Pragmatism, Process, and Religious Education." *Religious Education* 68:3 (May–June 1973): 322-31.

Fowler, James. *Stages of Faith.* San Francisco: Harper & Row, 1981.

Fowler, Jim, and Keen, Sam. *Life Maps: Conversations on the Journey of Faith.* Ed. Jerome Berryman. Waco, Tex.: Word Books, 1978.

Freire, Paulo. *Pedagogy of the Oppressed.* Trans. Myra Bergman Ramos. New York: Herder & Herder, 1970.

Fuchs, Ernst. *Studies of the Historical Jesus.* Trans. Andrew Scobie. Naperville, Ill.: Alec R. Allenson, 1964.

Gadamer, Hans-Georg. *Truth and Method.* New York: The Seabury Press, 1975.

Geiselmann, Joseph R. *The Meaning of Tradition*. New York: Herder & Herder, 1966.

Greene, Maxine. "Curriculum and Consciousness." In *Curriculum Theorizing,* ed. William Pinar. Berkeley: McCutchan, 1975.

Grimes, Howard. *The Church Redemptive*. Nashville: Abingdon Press, 1963.

Groome, Thomas. "The Critical Principle in Christian Education and the Task of Prophecy." *Religious Education* 72:3 (May–June 1977): 262-72.

———. "Christian Education: A Task of Present Dialectical Hermeneutics." *Living Light* 14:3 (Fall 1977): 408-23.

———. *Christian Religious Education: Sharing Our Story and Vision*. San Francisco: Harper & Row, 1980.

Gutiérrez, Gustavo. *A Theology of Liberation*. Maryknoll, N.Y.: Orbis Books, 1973.

Harris, Maria. "Word, Sacrament, Prophecy." In *Tradition and Transformation in Religious Education,* ed. Padraic O'Hare. Birmingham, Ala.: Religious Education Press, 1979.

Hartshorne, Charles. *Creative Synthesis and Philosophic Method*. La Salle, Ill.: Open Court Publishing Co., 1970.

Herbart, John Friedrich. *Outline of Educational Doctrine*. Trans. Alexis F. Lange. New York: The Macmillan Co., 1901.

Hofinger, Johannes. *The Art of Teaching Doctrine: The Good News and Its Proclamation*. Notre Dame, Ind.: University of Notre Dame Press, 1957.

———. *Our Message Is Christ*. Notre Dame, Ind.: Fides Publishers, 1974.

Holtz, Barry W. "Towards an Integrated Curriculum for the Jewish School." *Religious Education* 75:5 (September–October 1980): 546-57.

Huebner, Dwayne. "Curriculum as Concern for Man's Temporality." In *Curriculum Theorizing,* ed. William Pinar. Berkeley: McCutchan, 1975.

———. "The Language of Religious Education." In *Tradition and Transformation in Religious Education,* ed. Padraic O'Hare. Birmingham, Ala.: Religious Education Press, 1979.

Huesman, W. A., and Hofinger, J., eds., *The Good News Yesterday and Today*. New York: Sadlier, 1962.

Irwin, Paul. *The Care and Counseling of Youth in the Church*. Philadelphia: Fortress Press, 1975.

James, William. *The Varieties of Religious Experience*. New York: Longmans, 1925.

Jungmann, Josef A. *Announcing the Word of God.* Trans. Ronald Walls. New York: Herder & Herder, 1959.

———. *Handing on the Faith.* Trans. A. N. Fuerst. New York: Herder & Herder, 1959.

Kathan, Boardman W. "The Sunday School Revisited." *Religious Education* 75:1 (January–February 1980): 5-14.

Kaufman, Gordon. *God the Problem.* Cambridge: Harvard University Press, 1972.

Kimmel, Douglas C. *Adulthood and Aging.* New York: John Wiley & Sons, 1974.

Kliebard, Herbert. "Metaphorical Roots of Curriculum Design." In *Curriculum Theorizing,* ed. William Pinar. Berkeley: McCutchan, 1975.

Knoff, Gerald E. *The World Sunday School Movement.* New York: The Seabury Press, 1979.

Lang, Martin A. "Faith as a Learned Life-Style." In *Emerging Issues in Religious Education,* ed. Gloria Durka and Joanmarie Smith. Paramus, N.J.: Paulist/Newman Press, 1976.

Lee, Bernard. *The Becoming of the Church.* Paramus, N.J.: Paulist/Newman Press, 1974.

Lee, James Michael. *The Shape of Religious Instruction.* Birmingham, Ala.: Religious Education Press, 1971.

———. *The Flow of Religious Instruction.* Dayton: Pflaum Press, 1973.

Lifton, Robert Jay. "Protean Man." *Partisan Review* 35:1 (Winter 1968): 13-27.

Liturgy and Learning [issue theme]. *Religious Education* 74:6 (November–December 1979).

Lonergan, Bernard J. F. *Method in Theology.* London: Darton, Longman & Todd, 1972.

Lynn, Robert W., *Protestant Strategies in Education.* New York: Association Press, 1964.

Lynn, Robert W., and Wright, Elliott. *The Big Little School: Two Hundred Years of the Sunday School.* 2d ed. rev. and enl. Nashville: Abingdon; Birmingham, Ala.: Religious Education Press, 1980.

Macquarrie, John. *The Faith of the People of God.* New York: Charles Scribner's Sons, 1972.

———. *Principles of Christian Theology.* New York: Charles Scribner's Sons, 1977.

Mead, George Herbert. "Social Consciousness and the Consciousness of Meaning." *Psychological Bulletin* 7:12 (1910): 397-405.

————. "Scientific Method and Individual Thinker." In *Creative Intelligence,* ed. John Dewey et al. New York: Holt, Rinehart and Winston, 1917.

———— *The Philosophy of the Present.* LaSalle, Ill.: Open Court Publishing Co., 1932.

————. *Mind, Self, and Society: From the Standpoint of a Social Behaviorist.* Ed. Charles W. Morris. Chicago: University of Chicago Press, 1934.

————. *The Philosophy of the Act.* Ed. Charles W. Morris. Chicago: University of Chicago Press, 1938.

————. *The Social Psychology of George Herbert Mead.* Ed. Anselm Strauss. Chicago: University of Chicago Press, 1956.

Meland, Bernard E. *Higher Education and the Human Spirit.* Chicago: University of Chicago Press, 1953.

Miguez-Bonino, Jose. *Doing Theology in a Revolutionary Situation.* Philadelphia: Fortress Press, 1975.

Miller, Randolph Crump. *The Language Gap and God.* Philadelphia: Pilgrim Press, 1970.

Minear, Paul. *Images of the Church in the New Testament.* Philadelphia: The Westminster Press, 1972.

Moltmann, Jürgen. *Hope and Planning.* New York: Harper & Row, 1971.

————. Jürgen. *The Experiment Hope.* Philadelphia: Fortress Press, 1975.

————. *Theology of Hope.* New York: Harper & Row, 1967 (1975).

————. *The Invitation to an Open Messianic Life-Style Church.* Philadelphia: Fortress Press, 1978.

Moore, Allen. "The Place of Scientific Models and Theological Reflection in the Practice of Ministry." *Pastoral Psychology* 17:210 (January 1971): 25-34.

Nelson, C. Ellis. *Where Faith Begins.* Richmond: John Knox Press, 1967.

————. "Our Oldest Problem." In *Tradition and Transformation, in Religious Education,* ed. Padraic O'Hare. Birmingham, Ala.: Religious Education Press, 1979.

Neville, Gwen K., and Westerhoff, John H. *Learning Through Liturgy.* New York: The Seabury Press, 1978.

Ogden, Schubert. "What Is Theology?" *Journal of Religion* 52 (1972): 22-40.

O'Hare, Padraic, ed. *Tradition and Transformation in Religious Education.* Birmingham, Ala.: Religious Education Press, 1979.

Osterman, Mary Jo. "The Two Hundred Year Struggle for

Protestant Religious Education Curriculum Theory." *Religious Education* 75:5 (September–October 1980):528-38.

Palmer, Richard E. *Hermeneutics*. Evanston, Ill.: Northwestern University Press, 1969.

Pannenberg, Wolfhart. *The Apostles' Creed: In the Light of Today's Questions*. Philadelphia: The Westminster Press, 1972.

Perry, David W. *Homegrown Christian Education*. New York: The Seabury Press, 1979.

Peters, R. S. *Ethics and Education*. Glenview, Ill.: Scott, Foresman & Co., 1967, (1966).

Phenix, Philip. "Transcendence and the Curriculum." In *Curriculum Theorizing*, ed. William Pinar. Berkeley: McCutchan, 1975.

Pinar, William, ed. *Heightened Consciousness, Cultural Revolution, and Curriculum Theory*. Berkeley: McCutchan, 1974.

———. *Curriculum Theorizing*. Berkeley: McCutchan, 1975.

———. "Currere: Toward Reconceptualization." In *Curriculum Theorizing*. Berkeley: McCutchan, 1975.

Pittenger, Norman. *The Christian Church as Social Process*. Philadelphia: The Westminster Press, 1971.

Riegel, Klaus F. "Developmental Psychology and Society: Some Historical and Ethical Considerations." In *Life Span Development Psychology*, ed. J. R. Nesselroade and H. W Reese. New York: Academic Press, 1973.

———. "The Dialectics of Human Development." *American Psychologist* 31:10 (October 1976).

———. "Toward a Dialectical Theory of Development." *Human Development* 18 (1975):50-64.

———. "From Traits and Equilibrium Toward Developmental Dialectics." In *1974–75 Nebraska Symposium on Motivation*, ed. W. J. Arnold and J. K. Cole. Lincoln: University of Nebraska Press, 1976.

———. *Psychology of Development and History*. New York: Plenum, 1976.

Roberts, William L. "From Curriculum Research to Foundational Theorizing." *Religious Education* 75:5 (September–October 1980): 507-15.

Rose, Arnold M., ed. "A Systematic Summary of Symbolic Interaction Theory." In *Human Behavior and Social Processes*, ed. London: Routledge & Kegan Paul, 1962.

Russell, Letty. "Handing on Traditions and Changing the World." In *Tradition and Transformation in Religious Education*, ed.

Padraic O'Hare. Birmingham, Ala.: Religious Education Press, 1979.

Sanders, James. "Hermeneutics." In *Interpreter's Dictionary of the Bible Supplementary Volume,* ed. Keith Crim. Nashville: Abingdon, 1976.

———. "Adaptable for Life: The Nature and Function of Canon." In *Magnalia Dei: The Mighty Acts of God,* ed. F. M. Cross, W. E. Lemke, and P. D. Miller. Garden City, N.J.: Doubleday & Co., 1976.

———. "Hermeneutics in True and False Prophecy." In *Canon and Authority,* ed. George W. Coats and Burke O. Long. Philadelphia: Fortress Press, 1977.

Schleiermacher, Friedrich. *The Christian Faith.* Ed. H. R. Mackintosh and J. S. Stewart. 2 vols. New York: Harper & Row, 1963.

Segundo, Juan Luis. *The Community Called Church.* Trans. John Drufy. Maryknoll, N.Y.: Orbis Books, 1973.

Seymour, Jack. *From Sunday School to Church School: Continuities in Protestant Church Education, 1860-1929.* Washington, D.C., University Press of America, 1982.

Sherrill, Lewis. *The Rise of Christian Education.* New York: The Macmillan Co., 1953.

———. *The Gift of Power.* New York: The Macmillan Co., 1955.

Smith, H. Shelton. *Faith and Nurture.* New York: Charles Scribner's Sons, 1941.

Snyder, Ross. "A Ministry of Meanings." Mimeographed. Nashville: Youth Department, Division of the Local Church, General Board of Education of The Methodist Church, 1961.

———. "Educating a People of God." Mimeographed. Chicago: Chicago Theological Seminary, 1962.

———. "The Authentic Life: Its Theory and Practice." Mimeographed. Nashville: Older Youth–Young Adult Project, General Board of Education of The Methodist Church, 1963.

———. *Young People and Their Culture.* Nashville: Abingdon Press, 1969.

———. "Boisen's Understanding of Religious Experience." *Chicago Theological Seminary Register,* 67:1 (1977):33-51.

———. "A Lifetask of Senior Adulthood." Paper presented at the School of Theology at Claremont, February 1980.

Spirituality and Religious Education [issue theme]. *Religious Education,* 75:4 (July–August 1980).

Tillich, Paul. *Dynamics of Faith.* New York: Harper & Row, 1957.

Ulich, Robert. *History of Educational Thought*. New York: American Book Co., 1950.

Vernon, Walter N. "Curriculum Resources, Christian Nurture, and Changing Times." *Perkins Journal* 32:1 (Fall 1978): 8-13.

Vieth, Paul. *The Church and Christian Education*. St. Louis: Bethany Press, 1947.

Warford, Malcolm L. *The Necessary Illusion: Church, Culture and Educational Change*. Philadelphia: Pilgrim Press, 1976.

Westerhoff, John H. *Tomorrow's Church*. Waco, Tex.: Word Books, 1976.

———. *Will Our Children Have Faith?* New York: The Seabury Press, 1976.

Westerhoff, John H., and Neville, Gwen K. *Generation to Generation*. Philadelphia: Pilgrim Press, 1974.

Whitehead, Alfred North. *Religion in the Making*. New York: The Macmillan Co., 1926.

———. *Process and Reality*. New York: The Macmillan Co., 1957 (1929).

———. *The Aims of Education*. New York: The Free Press, 1967 (1929).

———. *Adventures of Ideas*. New York: The Free Press, 1933.

———. *Process and Reality*. Ed. David R. Griffin and Donald W. Sherburne. New York: The Free Press, 1978.

Wiles, Maurice. *What Is Theology?* London: Oxford University Press, 1976.

Williams, Daniel Day. *The Minister and the Care of Souls*. New York: Harper & Row, 1961.

Zisenwine, David. "Jewish Education—An Opportunity Model." *Religious Education* 75:5 (September–October 1980): 558-62.

Index

Aims, concept of, 150
Apostles' Creed, 163; and early church, 66
Applied theology, 71, 73
Appreciative consciousness, and Bernard Meland, 50
Authoritative revelation, problem of defining, 72

Bacon, Francis, 31
Barth, Karl, 37, 71, 72, 82
Behavioral objectives, 145
Behaviorists, 91
Betti, Emilio, 80
Bible: and Christian community, 60; and Christian education, 43; questioning authority of, 30; as record of human experience, 25
Biblical criticism, emergence of, 30
Biblical literalism, 162
Biblical tradition, and Ellis Nelson, 47
Boisen, Anton, 74
Bower Report, 40
Bower, William Clayton: and progressive religious education, 29-30, 31, 33, 53; and International Lesson Committee, 35
Boys, Mary, 28, 52, 53, 174; and dialogical theory, 49
Brave New World, 187
Browning, Don, 74
Brunner, Emil, 71
Bultmann, Rudolf, 80
Bushnell, Horace, 32

Calvin, John, 186
Campbell, Donald, 89

Canonical hermeneutics, and James Sanders, 81
Can Religious Education Be Christian? 41
Catechetical model: as deductive theological model, 73; as tradition-oriented education, 39
Change, 28, 87; as basic concept, 21; definition of, 22; education for, 63; education that maximizes, 163; integration of, with continuity, 115, 135; relationship of, with continuity, 94; teaching that facilitates, 163; in tension with continuity, 14; in thought of Whitehead, 103-6; and tradition, 23
Christian communities, and significant symbols, 165
Christian community: the accumulating wisdom of, 176-77; and change, 22; as community of mission, 67; as community of promise, 67, 82; in contemporary world, 14; continuity of, 21; continuity and change in, 18; difficulty in defining, 63; and experience, 24, 25; and ideals, 151; and knowledge, 133; life of, 61; the nature of, 156; preaching and teaching in, 66; in thought of John Westerhoff, 47; and tradition, 17, 23; as a traditioning community, 122, 138. *See also* Christian faith community; Community of faith; Faith community
Christian education, 28, 29; and communal context, 47; a dialogical model of, 48; integrating conti-